READWELL'S

LEARN URDU
IN A MONTH

**Easy Method of Learning Urdu
Through English Without a Teacher**

Compiled by
A.R. ZAKARIA
M.A.

Readwell Publications
New Delhi-110008

Published by:

READWELL PUBLICATIONS
B-8, Rattan Jyoti, 18, Rajendra Place
New Delhi-110 008 (INDIA)
Phone : 25737448, 25712649, 25721761
FAX : 91-11-25812385
E-mail : readwell@sify.com
newlight@vsnl.net

ISBN 81-87782-11-0

Printed at : Arya Offset Press, New Delhi.

PREFACE

Sometime ago while I was in search of a book on a science subject I chanced to see a book about which loud claims of learning a language in a short time without the aid of a teacher, were made. My curiosity knew no bounds and I wondered if it was possible to verify those claims. After reading a few pages here and there it took me no time to realise that this was a case of overestimation, not that this could not be done but because the book had many drawbacks. However, it prompted me to create a work myself which should be worthwhile and should really benefit the learner. Although I will not claim that one can master a language in a given period of time because language is a boundless thing, yet I have taken care to present my work in a simple and easy-to-understand manner. A beginner can follow the lessons without any pause and realise that this language is just not that difficult to learn as he had dreaded.

There are writters who ignore grammar and fill their books with translated sentences in the pious belief that one can learn a language with the aid of only readymade sentences. But this is wrong. Knowledge of grammar is essential for learning correct language. The superstructure of translations, howsoever well-mastered, just disappears as soon as the learner is asked to write grammatically correct

(iii)

sentences. The learner realises that he is nowhere near the language, and that the learning of grammar is basic to the learning of correct language. Once he understands the rules of grammar he has crossed more than half the way towards the learning of the language and easy presentation of these rules smoothens his path further.

-*Author*

A FEW WORDS

The chief object of this book is to meet a beginner's wants and to remove the difficulties which are not explained in most other books.

Points which to a learned writer may seem too easy to require an explanation, often present a great difficulty to a beginner.

When starting to learn Urdu a beginner has to face several difficulties, *e.g.:*

   (i)   The pronunciation;

  (ii)   The order of words in a sentence;

 (iii)   Formation of the various plurals;

 (iv)   Declensions of Noun;

  (v)   Agreement of the Adjectives and Verbs with the Nouns in gender, number and case.

At first read the Alphabet carefully, understanding the proper pronunciation from the given examples.

There are many *Ka, Sa* and *Za* in Urdu. You should know their differentiation of pronunciation. So read the examples carefully.

Read and write Urdu from right to left.

Read while you write (Read & write) is the best method for the beginners. So, you too write and at the same time read it.

To study the proper pronunciation and style of

speaking, listen to the programme of Urdu on Radio or T.V.

Read some simple story books and periodicals to further your knowledge.

In pronunciation be careful on vowels. The vowels of English language have more than one sound, but in Urdu every vowel has its own sound.

Before starting to write the Alphabet take the page headlines "How to write" and copy the letters giving attention to the white arrow marks inside the letters.

(a) At first study the letters from 'Alif' to 'Kha';
(b) Then start from 'Dall' upto 'Zhe';
(c) After that 'Seen' to 'Ghain';
(d) Lastly from 'Fe' to 'Ye';

Urdu letters have three forms of writing; study them as instructed above.

In Urdu there are signs for vowels.

(a) Study the signs of short vowels knowing the differences among these.
(b) Then study the signs of long vowels carefully.

CONTENTS

URDU ALPHABET: HOW TO WRITE

ALIF	BE	PE	TE
TA	SE	JEEM	CHE
HE	KHE	DAAL	DAAL

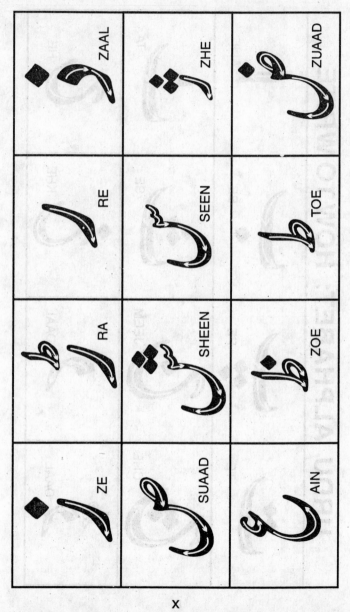

ZAAL	RE	RA	ZE
ZHE	SEEN	SHEEN	SUAAD
ZUAAD	TOE	ZOE	AIN

X

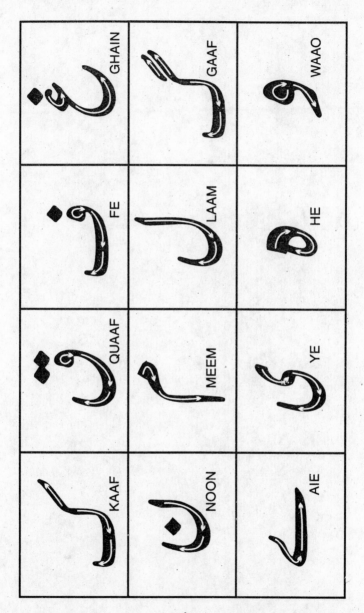

xi

LESSON 1
ALPHABET

alif be الف بے

Urdu Letters	Urdu Names	Pronunciation	Example
ا	Alif	a	as 'a' in far
ب	Be	b	as 'b' in big
پ	Pe	p	as 'p' in pen
ت	Te	t (Soft)	as 't' in three
ٹ	Ṭa	ṭ (Hard)	as 't' in toy
ث	Se	s (Arabic)	as 's' in sir
ج	Jeem	j	as 'j' in jar
چ	Che	ch	as 'ch' in child
ح	Ḥe	ḥ (Persian)	as 'h' in 'Mohal'
خ	Khe	kh (Guttural)	as 'ch' in loch
د	Daal	d (Soft)	as 'th' in the
ڈ	Ḍaal	ḍ (Hard)	as 'd' in dull
ذ	Zaal	z (Arabic)	as 'z' in Zikr
ر	Re	r	as 'r' in Rama
ڑ	Ṛa	ṛ (Hard)	as 'r' in Larka

1

ز	*ze*	z	as 'z' in zoo
ژ	*zhe*	zh	as 'z' in lizard
س	*seen*	s	as 's' in sun
ش	*sheen*	sh	as 'sh' in shine
ص	*suaad*	ṣ (Persian)	as 's' in 'soorat'
ض	*zuaad*	ẓ (Persian)	as 'z' in 'zarur'
ط	*toe*	ṭ (Arabic)	as 't' in 'tarah'
ظ	*zoe*	ẓ (Arabic)	as 'z' in 'nazar'
ع	*ain*	a (Arabic)	Guttural
غ	*ghain*	gh (Guttural)	as 'g' in sagen
ف	*fe*	f	as 'f' in fee
ق	*quaaf*	q (Guttural)	as 'q' in 'qalam'
ک	*kaaf*	k	as 'c' in calf
گ	*gaaf*	g	as 'g' in go
ل	*laam*	l	as 'l' in long
م	*meem*	m	as 'm' in me
ن	*noon*	n	as 'n' in name
و	*waao*	w,o,u,	as in English
ہ	*he*	h	as 'h' in hot
ی	*ye*	e	*as 'a' in late*

2

EXERCISE

RECOGNISE THE LETTERS

ا د س ع ل ی ج

ب چ ڈ ش غ م ے

پ ح ذ ص ف ن ت

خ ر ض ق و ٹ ڑ گ

ہ ش ء ز ط ک ظ

ح ع ص س ا ر ڈ ڑ ٹ

ل ک گ ے ت ق

ب ج و ہ ث ش

غ خ ن ظ ف ذ پ چ

3

Vowel-Sounds and their Transliteration	Initial		Non-Initial	
اَ = a as *a* in *ago* or *u* in *but*	اَب	*ab*	مَل	*mal*
آ = a as *a* in *father, rather, transfer*	آب	*aab*	مال	*maal*
اِ = i as *i* in *sin*	اِس	*is*	مِل	*mil*
ئی = ee as *ee* in *seek, feel*	اِیخ	*eekh*	میل	*meel*
اُ = u as *u* in *full*	اُس	*us*	مُل	*mul*
اُو = u as *u* in *rude* or as *oo* in *fool*	اُون	*oon*	مول	*mool*
ے = e as *e* in *pale*	اے	*ek*	مے	*mel*
اَے = ae as *a* in *at, man, gap,* and *have*	اَیسا	*aesa*	مَیل	*mael*
او = o as *o* in *note, more*	اوس	*os*	مول	*mol*
او = au as *au* in *auto*	اور	*aur*	مول	*maul*

TYPICAL USAGE OF DETACHED FORM

Name	Detached Form	Transliteration and Pronunciation	Name	Detached Form	Transliteration and Pronunciation
Alif	ا	A, as A in far	Khē	خ	Kh guttural, as Ch in Loch
Bē	ب	B, as in English	Dāl	د	D soft, as Th in They
Pē	پ	P, as in English	Dāl	ڈ	D hard, as D in Dog
Tē	ت	T, a soft dental like in three	Zāl	ذ	Z, like Z in Zoo
Ta	ٹ	T, hard as T in Tin-tack	Rē	ر	R, as in English
Sē	ث	S, as S in sit	Rē	ڑ	Re, a hard R.
Jeem	ج	J, like J in Jail	Zē	ز	Z, as in English
Chē	چ	Ch, as Ch in Church	Zhē	ژ	Zh, as in Azure
Hē	ح	H, like H in Huge	Seen	س	S like S in Sun.

5

| | Detach-ed Form | Transliteration and Pronunciation | | Detach-ed Form | Transliteration and Pronunciation |
Name			Name		
Sheen	ش	Sh, as Sh in Shut	Kāf	ک	K, as in English
Suād	ص	S, as S in Sit	Gāf	گ	G, as G in Give
Zuād	ض	Z, as Z in Zeal	Lām	ل	L, as L in Lane
Toē	ط	T, as T in Tie	Meem	م	M, as in English
Zoē	ظ	Z, as Z in Zebra	Noon	ن	N, as in English
Ain	ع	A, guttural (consonant)	Wāo	و	W,O,U, as in English
Ghain	غ	Gh, as G in the German word Sagen.	Hē	ہ	H, as H in Hot
Fē	ف	F, as F in Fun	Yē	ی	Y, as in Yard
Quaf	ق	Q, guttural, like Ck in Stuck	Yē	ے	E, as Ey in They

6

DIFFERENT FORMS OF LETTERS

All letters, with a few exceptions, have four forms, *i.e.,* initial, medial, final and independent. The independent form is also called 'the Detached Form'. To write a word all the letters used are joined to one another. The essential part of the letter, however remains unchanged as is shown here:

Detached form	initial	medial	final
ب	بـ	ـيـك	لب

Detached Form

ث	ٹ	ت	پ	ب	ا	
ذ	ڈ	د	خ	ح	چ	ج
ش	س	ژ	ز	ڑ	ر	
غ	ع	ظ	ط	ض	ص	
ن	م	ل	گ	ک	ق	ف
ے	ی	ہ	و			

7

Initial Form

To obtain the initial form strike off the horizontal lines and circles of the detached form, as,

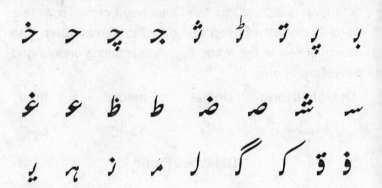

IMPORTANT: Since the following nine letters have neither a circle nor a horizontal line they do not change except in the case of the final form. They are always joined to the preceding letter, but not to the one following. All letters when used after them are written in the initial or detached form as the case may be.

و   ژ   ز   ڑ   ر   ذ   ڈ   د   ا

Medial Form

The medial form is obtained by adding a connecting line to the right side of the initial form, as,

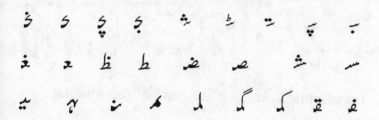

Final Form

The final form is obtained by adding the same connecting line to the beginning of the detached form.

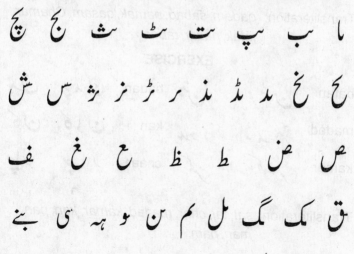

EXERCISE

Read and copy the following words:

sab	سب	سب	jab	جب جب	جب
bas	بس	بس	ham	ہم	ہم
das	دس	دس	khat	خط خط	خط

Transliteration : *kab, jab, rab, das, nal, gaz, khat, tal.*

sabaq	سبق	سبق	safar	سفر سفر	سفر
qadam	قدم	قدم	qalam	قلم قلم	قلم
namak	نمک نمک	نمک	qasam	قسم قسم	قسم

Transliteration: *qadam, sabaq, namak, qasam, Chaman,*
latak, nazar, rabar.

EXERCISE

batan	بٹن	بٹن	badan	بدن بدن	بدن
madad	مدد مدد	مدد	kan	کان کان	کان
kamar	کمر کمر	کمر	chaar	چار چار	چار

Transliteration: *sat, taj, char, madad, kamar, kan, pan,*
man, nam.

10

LESSON 2

PRONUNCIATION

ا *alif* at the commencement of a word is a mere prop for the letter 'hamza' and has no sound of itself.

2. ت and د (te and dal) are softer and more dental than their English equivalents 'T' and 'D'; the tip of the tongue should touch the upper front teeth when these letters are pronounced.

3. ر re is pronounced distinctly like the French 'r'.

4. ڑ Re has a heavy sound and when pronouncing it, the tip of the tongue must be turned much farther back.

5. ث s, س s, ص s are Urdu homophones. They are all pronounced like 's' in sit.

6. ج 'G', is always pronounced as 'g' in 'germ' and never as 'g' in 'game'.

7. چ '<u>Ch</u>' is pronounced as 'ch' in 'church' and not as 'ch' in 'chorus'.

8. ح h is often pronounced like 'h' but should be more guttural than the 'h' in huge.

9. ذ z, ز z, ض z, ظ z are Urdu homophones and are pronounced like the 'z' in zeal.

11

10. ع (*Ain*) is a strong guttural (consonant).

11. غ 'gh' is a guttural 'g' accompanied by a rattling. The 'g' in the French grasseye is an approximation only.

12. ق 'q' is a strong guttural, like the 'ck' in stuck when pronounced in the throat.

13. ه 'h' as in hand.

PRONUNCIATION OF VOWELS

'a'	is	pronounced	as	'a'	in	Mental
'a'	"	"	"	'a'	"	Part
'ai'	"	"	"	'a'	"	Bank
'au'	"	"	"	'au'	"	Paul
'e'	"	"	"	'e'	"	Prey
'i'	"	"	"	'i'	"	Pit
'i'	"	"	"	'i'	"	Fatigue
'o'	"	"	"	'o'	"	Home
'u'	"	"	"	'u'	"	Put
'ū'	"	"	"	'u'	"	June

12

SHORT VOWELS

There are three short vowels: *Zabar* (◌َ) *Zer* (◌ِ) and *Pesh* (ؤ) which in English are represented by a short "a", short "i" and short "u" respectively. *In practice they are seldom written or printed.*

Zabar   To express the short "a" zabar is used over a letter as *ba* بَ, *na* نَ, *par* پَ and is pronounced like the "u" in the English word "gun",

moment	*pal*	نَپل	پَل
grief	*gham*	غَم	غَم
all	*sab*	سَب	سَب
armpit	*baghal*	اَغَل	بَغَل
eye brow	*palak*	پَلَکَ	پَلَگ

Zer   The short "i" is expressed by using *zer* under a letter, as *khi* خِ, *li* لِ. It is pronounced as "i" in "fin".

heart	*dil*	دِل	دِل
pin	*pin*	پِن	پِن
day	*din*	دِن	دِن

13

| what | kiā | کیا | کیا |
| Book | kitāb | کتاب | کتاب |

Pesh. Similarly, the short "u" is expressed by putting a *pesh* over a letter, as mu, ju, and is pronounced like the "u" in "put".

bridge	pul	پُل	پُل
you	tum	تُم	تُم
God	Khuda	خُدا	خُدا
Sun	Sūraj	سُورج	سُورج
bad	burā	بُرا	بُرا

EXERCISE

Transliteration: pal, ghap, gham, hal, samar, badan, kān, sāg, bāgh, chāl, jo, so, gir, sir, Khudā, kitāb, kia, tum, din, dil, sāt, nāch, shān.

LONG VOWELS

1. *Alif* ا , *Wāo* و and *Ye* ی are used in Urdu as long vowels.

2. *Alif* ا gives the sound of 'aa' and mostly used in initial form.

3. *Wao* و gives the sound of 'w', au, u, and o, whereas ye ی stands for y, ai, i, and e.

4. When و and ی are used at the beginning of a word or syllable it gives the sound of 'w', and 'y' as

   wahshat   وحشت   yaklakht يكلخت

EXAMPLE

Initial	Medial	Final
ا o, as, اُس os	و o, as, موٹا motā	لُو lo
اَو au, as, اَور aur	وَ au, as, فَوج fauj	جَو jau
اُو ū, as, اُون ūn	وُ u, as, خُوب khūb	چاقُو chāqū
اِء e, as, اِلْچی Elchī	یہ e, as, میں mēn	ے e, ے as, بڑے bare
اَء ai, as, ایسا aisā	یٔ ai, as, مَیں main	ے ai, as, ہے hai
اِء i, as, اِیجاد ijad	یٖ i as, یقین yaqin	ی i, as, لڑکی larki

EXERCISE

Read and copy the following:

حَوض ۔ فَوج ۔ گَونٔ ۔ چَوک ۔ اَوٗر ۔ خَوف ۔ پَیر ۔

سَیر ۔ بَیل ۔ لے ۔ نے ۔ خَیر ۔ بَیر ۔ ایک ۔ جیب ۔ دیگ ۔

دیر ۔ بیر ۔ سبب ۔ شیر ۔ بُول ۔ توپ ۔ ڈُول ۔

مُور ۔ شُور ۔ اُوس ۔ سُوچ ۔ سُورج ۔ چُوڑی ۔ مُولی ۔ آلو ۔

بَابُو ۔ چاقُو ۔ خَالُو ۔ جُوتا ۔ چُونا ۔ مُورَت ۔ صُورت ۔

Transliteration: *Hauz, fauj, mauj, kaun, chauk, aur, khauf, pair, sair, bail, ley, ney, khair, bair, ēk, jèb, dèg, dèr, bèr, sēb, shèr, bol, top, dol, mor, shor, os, soch, sūraj, mūli, ālū, bàbū, chāqū, khàlū, jūtā, chūnà, mūrat, sūrat.*

15

LESSON 3

THE METHOD OF WRITING URDU

To write a word, the letters are joined to one another, as the case may be:

PRONUNCIATION->		WORD	<---SPELLING--->
		قلم	ق ل م
PEN	qalam	m la qa	meem laam quaaf
		سفر	س ف ر
TRAVEL	safar	r fa sa	re fe seen
		شہر	ش ہ ر
TOWN	shahar	r ha sha	re he sheen
		مشعل	م ش ع ل
TORCH	mashal	l a sha ma	laam ain sheen meem
		گرم	گ ر م
WARM	garam	m ra ga	meem re gaaf
		بدن	ب د ن
BODY	badan	n da ba	noon daal be
		بچپن	ب پ چ ن
CHILDHOOD	bachpan	n pa ch ba	noon pe che be
		بکواس	ب ک و ا س
GOSSIP	bakwaas	s waa k ba	seen alif waao kaaf be
		فقط	ف ق ط
SIMPLY	faqt	t q fa	toe quaaf fe

16

SHORT WORDS

NOW	ab	ا ب a b
GOD	rab	ر ب ra b
BREATH	dam	د م da m
TEN	das	د س da s
GOLD	zar	ز ر za r
RESPECT	adab	ا د ب a da b
PAIN	dard	د ر د da r d
PAGE, LEAF	waraq	و ر ق wa r q
INKSTAND	dawaat	د و ا ت da wa a t
STOP	ruk	ر ک ru k
TAIL	dum	د م du m

17

INTELLECT	aqal	عقل l qa a	ل ق ع laam quaaf ain
SIMPLY	faqt	فقط t q fa	ف ق ط toe quaaf fa
TOMORROW/ YESTERDAY	kal	کل l ka	ک ل laam kaaf
CHAT	bakwaas	بکواس s waa k ba	ب ک و ا س seen alif waa kaaf ba
STEP	pag	پگ g pa	پ گ gaaf pe
THEN	tab	تب b ta	ت ب be te
OFTEN	aksar	اکثر r sa k a	ا ک ث ر re se kaaf alif
THAT	us	اُس s u	ا س seen pesh alif
ALL	sab	سَب b sa	سَ ب be seen
WHEN	jab	جَب b ja	جَ ب be jeem

18

		شک	ش ک
DOUBT	shak	k sha	kaaf sheen
		مِل	م ِ ل
MEET	mil	l mi	laam zer meem
		گِر	گ ِ ر
FALL	gir	r gi	re zer gaaf
		گُم	گ ُ م
HIDDEN	gum	m gu	meem pesh gaaf
		تُم	ت ُ م
YOU	tum	m tu	meem pesh te
		بَدن	ب د ن
BODY	badan	n da ba	noon daal be
		خُدا	خ ُ د ا
GOD	khudaa	a d khu	alif daal pesh khe

EXERCISE

Read and write the following:-

آن۔ آس۔ آب۔ آج۔ آٹا۔ آغا۔ آقا۔ آنا۔ آگ۔ آم۔
آج آپ کیا کر رہے ہیں؟   جب تک سانس تب تک آس۔ آٹا نہیں ہے۔
آرا کہاں ہے؟ آگ جل رہی ہے۔ یہ آم خراب ہے۔ آدمی بازار میں ہے۔

Transliteration: - ām, ānā, āg, āqā, āp, ān, ās, āj, ārā,
ātā, ālu.

19

Read and copy the following:-

مُرغ۔ فَرش۔ شَمع۔ کِرچ۔ مِرچ۔ عِلم۔ جِسم۔ گَرم۔ سَبز۔ سَرد۔ سُرخ۔

سُرخ مِرچ تیز ہوتی ہے۔ موسم سَرد ہے۔ فَرش گیلا ہے۔ شَمع خاموش ہے۔ عِلم بڑی نعمت ہے۔ اُس کا جِسم گَرم ہے۔ سِپاہی کے پاس تلوار ہے۔

Transliteration: *farsh, shama, garm, sabz, sard, sūrkh, ilm, mirch, jism.*

سوئی۔ کوئی۔ کئی۔ گئی۔ آؤ۔ جاؤ۔ چباؤ۔ سُناؤ۔ دیئے۔ لئے۔ چائے۔ گائے۔ دائیں۔ بائیں۔

Transliteration: *gāē, chāē, tāsīr, fāeda, kayī, gayi, judāī, gūnjāīsh.*

Read and copy the following:

بھوک۔ پھل۔ پھُول۔ چھڑی۔ جھاڑو۔ تھیلا۔ ٹھیلا۔ مَکئی کا بھٹّا۔ ریل کا ٹھیلا۔ زَہرہ کا بھائی۔ رَتن کی جھاڑو۔ مَداری کا تھیلا۔ گُلاب کا پھُول۔ زُور کی بھوک۔ احمد کا جھُولا۔ اِبا کی چھڑی۔ آم کا پھل۔ اَمجد کی چھتری۔ آپا کا جھُومر۔ پیتل کی دیگچی۔

20

ASPIRATED CONSONANTS

بھ	bh as,	بھالو bhālū	دھ	dh as,	دَھم dham
پھ	ph as,	پھُول phūl	ڈھ	dh as,	ڈھال dhāl
تھ	th as,	تھال thāl	ڑھ	rh as,	گڑھ garh
ٹھ	th as,	ٹھیلا thelā	کھ	kh as,	کھانا khana
جھ	jh as,	جھُول jhol	گھ	gh as,	گھر ghar
چھ	chh as,	چھری chhurī	لھ	lh as,	دولھا dūlhā

EXERCISE

دَس تک گِنو ۔ آج کیا دن ہے؟ ۔ گلاس دے آؤ ۔ لڑ کی پانی لائی ۔
کل عید ہے ۔ یہ نیم کا پیڑ ہے ۔ ریل چلتی ہے ۔ بادل گرجتا ہے ۔ بجلی چمکتی
ہے ۔ مور ناچتا ہے ۔ مُوتی آیا ہے ۔ طوطا بولتا ہے ۔ شور نہ کیجئے ۔ بُلبُل کا نغمہ
سُنئے ۔ ہُد ہُد اُڑ گیا ۔ اُستاد کا ادب کرو ۔ خُدا سے دُعا کرو ۔ یہ ایک
مُورت ہے ۔ کیسی خُوب صُورت ہے ۔ وہ سُورج نکلا ۔ ریل آتی ہَے ۔
سانپ کا تماشہ ہو رہا ہے ۔ دانت صاف کر ۔ مینہہ خُوب برسا ۔ حوض کا
پانی صاف ہے ۔ وہ اَنگُور کی بیل ہے ۔ یہ گلاب کا پَودا ہَے ۔ شمع روشن
کرو ۔ پانی گرم ہے ۔ گشتی چپّو سے چلتی ہے ۔ چلّو میں پانی لو ۔ حجام
سے بال کٹوالو ۔

21

LESSON 4

FORMING WORDS

ا

Alif ا is the first letter of Urdu alphabet. It is pronounced according to the vowel point (*erab*) which accompanies it; for example:

اَ *alif* with *zabar* sounds as the English *"a"* in *"large"*.

اِ *alif* with *zer* sounds as the English *"i"* in *"sin"*;

اُ *alif* with *pesh* sounds as the English *"u"* in "full";

آ *alif* with *mud* sounds as the English *"aa"*.

ا is always used in its full form. It is never joined when it occurs in the beginning of a word, *i.e.*, in a word beginning with ا . It is written separately and not joined to the next letter. It is joined with other letters only when it occurs after them, and it is joined in its full form. It will be further explained later while dealing with other letters.

Examples:

Now	ub	اب	=	ب	+	ا
This	is	اس	=	س	+	اِ
Them	un	ان	=	ن	+	اُ
Today	aaj	آج	=	ج	+	آ

22

ث ٹ ت پ ب

Note the similarity in these letters. The main body is the same; only the number and location of dots, called *noqta* make the difference. So, when these letters are joined with other letters, they adopt similar forms. But the form itself varies. These letters adopt the following different forms.

(i) They adopt the form of a small semicircle like this ‍ٮ and the dots are placed as required. For example:

ژ ڑ ڗ پ ٮ

These letters adopt this form when they occur in the beginning or in the middle of a word. For example:

ب+ا=با، ب+ا=باٹ، پ+ا=پان

ٹ+ب=ٹب، ٹ+ا=ٹاٹ، ب+ن=بٹن

(ii) They adopt the form of a thick tick like this ⁄ and the dots are placed as usual. Again, they adopt this form when they occur in the beginning of a word but only when followed by

ج- چ- ح- خ- م

For example:

بم=م+ب، ، بح=ح+ب، بچ=چ+ب، ، بج=ج+ب

23

(iii) These letters adopt yet another form which is like half of ل like this ﻟ. Usually this form is used when and of these letters occurs in the beginning of a word and followed by—

س ـ ش ـ ص ـ ض ـ ط ـ ظ ـ ع ـ غ ـ ف ـ ق ـ و

For example:

بـ + س = بس ، بـ + ش = بش ، بـ + ط = بط

ٹـ + ف = ٹف ، بـ + ق = بق ، پـ + ف = پف

بـ + و + ت + ل = بوتل

(iv) These letters are written in their original and perfect forms when they occur at the end of a word, that is, when a word ends in any of these letters, they adopt their perfect forms. For example:

اب ـ آپ ـ تب ـ تاب ـ بت

You should not be confused by the different forms of these letters. They are used only to help the writer in joining them with other letter. A little practice will help you a lot. In fact, it simplifies writing and makes it faster. The dots are always there for the identification of the actual letter. You are saved from the strain of remembering too many faces of letters.

ج ۔ چ ۔ ح ۔ خ

These four letters are similar in form. The number and position of dots indicate the difference. Apart from the dots, these letters consist of two main parts, that is, the head and the semicircle.

These letters are written in their perfect forms when they occur at the end of a word; for example:

آج ۔ تاج ۔ باج ۔ راج ۔ تارج ۔ چ ۔ خ

Only the head with a small portion of the neck like this ٢ with appropriate number of dots is used when any of these letters come in the beginning or in the middle of a word; for example:

ج + ا = جا، ج + ب = جب، ج + ح = جح، ج + ح = جح،
چ + ل = چل، ح + ل = حل، خ + ط = خط، چ + ک = چک

د ڈ ذ

These three letters, similar in form, are written as they are when a word begins with any one of them. They are not joined to any other letter following them as is the case with ا . They are written separately in the beginning;

25

for example:

دَف۔ ڈُل۔ دِل۔ ذَرّہ۔ ذَرَا

ڈال ۔ دال

They are joined with other letters only when they follow them. In doing so their head portion is trimmed, that is, only the lower portion, which is very much like د , is added; for example:

ب + د = بد، ج + د + ا = جدا

خ + د + ا = خدا

ر ڈ ز

This is another set of similar letters. Their position is very much similar to those of د ڈ ذ , that is, they are written separately when a word begins with any of them. Their shape is slightly changed when joined with other letters preceding them.

No word begins with ڑ

Examples:

رَب۔ رُخ۔ رَس۔ رِش۔ زَر۔ زَرد۔ ذات

26

The upper portion of these letters is slightly elongated and crooked when joined with preceding letters.

Examples:

خ + ر = خر، چ + ر + ج = چرج،

چ + ر + خ = چرخ، ٹ + ر + ک = ٹرک

Note 1: No alphabet is joined after

ا۔ د ڈ ذ۔ ر ڑ ز۔ و

Note 2: ا۔ د ڈ ذ۔ ر ڑ ز۔ و are never joined when preceded or followed by each other.

These two letters consist of two main parts, the trident head and the semicircle. For facility in writing a long slanting curve may be used instead of the trident.

These two letters are written in full when they occur at the end of a word.

Examples:

ب + س = بس، ر + ش = رش، ج + س = جس،

پ + س = پس، ج + و + ش = جوش، پ + ا + س = پاس،

خ + س = خس

When these two letters occur in the beginning or in the middle of a word only the first half, that is, the trident or the slanting curve head is written and the remaining portion is dropped.

Examples:

سـ + ب = سب، شـ + ب = شب، سـ + ج = سَج،

سـ + ل = سِل، شـ + ل = شَل، جـ + سـ + م = جِسم، چـ + ش + م = چَشم

ص ض

ص ـ ض , like س ـ ش are written in full when they occur at the end of word and only the top portion is written when they occur in the beginning or in the middle of a word.

Examples:

بـ + ص = بَص ـ حـ + ص = حَص ـ صـ + بـ + ح = صُبح ـ

ضـ + د = ضِد ـ ضـ + ل = ضَل

ط ظ

These two letters are always written as they are, wherever they may occur. Examples:

بـ + ط = بَط ـ ط + بـ = طِب ـ ظ + ر + ف = ظَرف

ط + و + ر = طور

28

غ ـ ع

Each of these two letters consists of two main parts, that is, the parrot-like head and the semicircle.

ع is pronounced differently with *zabar, zer* and *pesh* as is the case of *alif*.

(a) When a word begins with ع or غ, the semicircle is dropped as is the case of ج چ ح خ س ش or ض ص. Only the head is written when a word begins with ع or غ.

Examples:

ع + شہ + ق = عِشق، غو + و + ر = غَور، غو + م = غَم

غو + ل = غُل

(b) In the middle of a word also only the head of ع or غ is written. But here the head itself adopts a different form which is very much like a thick dash with a small neck like this ﻌ.

Examples:

بہ + عہ + ض = بَعض، شہ + عہ + ر = شِعر، شہ + بغ + ل = شَغل

بہ + غہ + ل = بَغل

(c) ع غ are written in full but with a blunt dash-like head when they occur at the end of a word but not separatey.

29

Examples:

ر + ب + ع = رَبع، سـ + ب + ع = سَبع

(d) ع غ are written in their original form when they occur at the end of a word and not joined.

Examples:

بـ + ا + غ = باغ، چ + ر + ا + غ = چِراغ، شـ + ا + ر + ع = شارع

ف ق

These two letters are written in full when they come at the end of a word, as is the case of many other letters.

Examples:

دَ + ف = دَف، دِ + ق = دِق۔ حـ + ق = حَق، صـ + ا + ف = صَاف

Only the head with the suitable number of dots, as the case may be, is written when ق ف occur in the *beginning* or in the *middle* of a word.

Examples:

فـ + ر + ق = فَرق، قـ + حـ + ط = قَحط، فـ + تـ + ح = فَتح

قـ + ا + ش = قاش

ک گ

This is another set of similar letters. ک and گ are written in their perfect forms when a word ends in any of them.

30

Examples:

باک ۔ پاک ۔ جگ ۔ شَنگ

ک and گ are written in an imperfect form when
they occur in the beginning or in the middle of a word *but
not followed by* ا or ل. In that case the length of their
lower part is slightly trimmed.

Examples:

ک + ب = کب ۔ ک + س = کس ۔ ک + ش = کَش ۔ گ + م = گُم

ک + ج = کج

ک and گ take a completely different form when
they are added before ا and ل. This form of ک and
گ consists of a small circle and one slanting tick over it
in case of ک and two similar ticks in case of گ.

Examples:

ک + ا + ج = کاج ۔ گ + ا + م = گام ۔ ک + ل = کل ۔ گ + ل = گل

ل

ل is written in full when a word ends with it.

Examples:

دِل ۔ سِل ۔ کاجل

ل is written in an imperfect form like this ﻟ, a seg-
ment of the lower semicircle being dropped, when ل is

31

joined in the beginning or in the middle.

Examples:

ر + ب = لَب ۔ کا + لُ + ج = کالُج ۔ با + لُ + ش = بالِش ۔

Note: ل+ا is written as لا and it is regarded as a compound letter, called *lam-alif*.

Examples:

اُجلا ۔ چَلا ۔ بولا

م

م is written in its perfect form when a word ends in م.

Examples:

ک + م = گَم ۔ ت + م = تُم ۔ ق + س + م = قِسَم

Only the first half of م , that is, the head is written when م occurs in the beginning or in the middle of a word.

Examples:

م + کا + ن = مَکان۔ م + چا + ن = مُچان۔ چ + م + ن = چَمن

ن

ن is written in its perfect form when a word ends in ن.

Examples:

ا + م + ن = اَمن، ر + س + ن = رسن، وَطن، وَ + ط + ن، دَ + ا + م + ن = دَامن

When ن occurs in the beginning or in the middle of a word it is written ن, just as ب پ ت ٹ ث are written; that is, in the form of a small semicircle. A dot in the semicircle will differentiate it from other letters.

Examples:

نب ۔ نل ۔ ناک ۔ اَناج

When ن occurs before م خ ح چ ج takes the form of a thick tick, as in the case of ب پ ت ٹ ث .

Examples:

نج ۔ اَنجان ۔ نِجس ۔ نَم ۔ خانَم

Again, as like ب پ ت ٹ ث take the form ب before

س ش ص ض ط ظ ع غ ف ق و

ن also takes a similar form with a dot above, before these letters.

Examples:

نَس ۔ نُطق ۔ نَقل ۔ بانو

NASAL SOUND OF ن (Nun Ghunna) i.e., ں

In many words ن is used to make a nasal sound. In such case the dot of ن is dropped. And a nasal sound occurs only in the end of a word.

Examples:-

ماں ۔ کلاں ۔ کارواں

33

Note: The dot in *Nun Ghunnā* is written when nasal sound occurs in the middle of a word.

Examples:

رَنگ۔ اَنگ۔ سانپ۔ ٹانگ۔

When ن occurs before ب in certain cases, it gives the sound of م .

Examples:

mamba منبَع   *dumba* دُنبہ

و

و gives the vowel sounds of O and U and consonant sounds of V and W. و is always written in its full form. It is always joined after a letter and *never* before a letter. It is always written separately if a word begins with و, as in the case of ١ .

و is never joined with ١۔ د ڈ ذ۔ ر ڑ ز

Examples of vowel sounds:

ب+و+ل=بول۔ چ+و+ر= چور۔ ط+و+ل=طول

Examples of consonant sounds:

سِ+و+ا+ر=سَوار۔ و+ر+م=وَرم۔ و+ر+ق=وَرق

Note: و is silent in some words. It is written but not pronounced.

Examples:

Desire *Qahish* خواہش   Dream *Khab* خواب

34

This letter is written in various forms which you will have to learn by practice.

(a) ہ adopts its original form and it is written separately when it comes at the end of a word and it is preceded by ‌ا۔ د ڈ ذ۔ ر ڑ ز ۔ و

Examples:

راہ۔ وہ۔ پُرزہ۔ بَندہ

(b) In some cases ہ is written like this ﮭ and an inverted comma is inserted under it, like this ﮭ .

Examples:

ب + ہ + ا+ر = بَہار۔ پ + ہ + ا+ڑ = پہاڑ۔ س + ہ + ل = سہل

(c) Sometimes ہ gives a soft sound, very much similar to a short sound of ا . In such cases ہ is written like this ﮨ without the inverted comma underneath.

Examples:

ت + و + ب + ﮨ = توبہ۔ خ + و + ش + ﮨ = خوشہ۔ ص + ف + ح + ﮨ = صفحہ

(d) ہ is written in the form of a small semicircle with an inverted comma underneath, in some cases, like this ﮩ .

Examples:

ہوا۔ ہودہ۔ ہل

35

(e) There is a very important use of ہ in Urdu. It is written in the form of two eyes like this ھ and called *do chashmi hay* (meaning the 'hay' like two eyes). Several letters are joined with this form of ھ to make compound letters.

Examples:

چھال، بھوت، گھوڑا، جھولا

Hamza ء is more or less like English 's' in form. It is more a vowel sign than a letter. No word begins with *Hamza*. Its vowel sound is very close to that of 'i' . ء is generally placed over a letter. In most of such cases an extra part of a letter has to be written and ء is made over it. This extra part of a letter takes form similar to those of ث ٹ ت پ ب when they are joined with different letters.

Examples:

Assistant	*nāeb*	نائب	Able	*laeq*	لائق
Results	*natāej*	نتائج			

When ء is to be written over و no addition of the extra portion is necessary. Simply make a ء over the و, such as:

Boat	*nāo*	ناؤ	Injury	*ghāo*	گھاؤ

ء is written with ا in some words, for example:

The rich	*umra*	امراء	The poor	*fuqra*	فقراء

36

ی ے

These are two principal forms of the last alphabet. 'ye' ی is used as a vowel to produce the sound of 'i' or 'ee', ے (bari ye) is used to produce the sound of 'ey' or 'ay'. These two principal forms are used when ی or ے occurs at the end of a word.

Examples:

آدمی ۔ ہنسی ۔ کرنسی ۔ لمبے ۔ بڑے ۔ منگے

ی ے With Other LETTERS

With ب پ ت ٹ ث ۔ ن : When a word ends in ی or ے and is preceded by any of these letters. ی or ے is written in its principal form. But in the process of writing the head is slightly trimmed and these letters themselves are written in a bracket-like form, like this ں , with suitable dots above or below as the case may be.

Example:

آ + ب + ی = آبی ۔ پا + ن + ی = پانی

Wtih ل : ی or ے preceded by ل is trimmed as explained above and ل itself takes the half form.

Examples:

نا + ل + ی = نالی ۔ جا + ل + ی = جالی ۔ کا + ل + ے = کالے ۔ تا + ل + ے = تالے

COMPOUND LETTERS

It has already been stated that *do-chashmi hay* ھ is joined with several other letters to form compound letters. You should not be confused, as it is mere combination of letters, thoroughly explained, with ھ.

NOTE: Read the following examples carefully.

bh بھ = ھ + ب :-

| Steam | *bhāp* | بھاپ | India | *Bhārat* | بھارت |
| Now | *abhi* | ابھی | Ever | *kabhī* | کبھی |

ph پھ = ھ + پ :-

| Fruit | *phal* | پھل | Flower | *phūl* | پھول |
| Torn | *phatā* | پھٹا | Gallows | *phansi ka Takhta* | پھانسی کا تختہ |

th تھ = ھ + ت :-

| Plate | *thālī* | تھالی | Spittle | *thūk* | تھوک |
| Hand | *hāth* | ہاتھ | Forehead | *māthā* | ماتھا |

chh چھ = ھ + چ :-

| Daggar | *chhurā* | چھرا | Umbrella | *chhatrī* | چھتری |
| Calf | *bachhrā* | بچھڑا | Skin | *chhilkā* | چھلکا |

dh دھ = ھ + د :-

| Dust | *dhool* | دھول | Warning | *dhamki* | دھمکی |
| Half | *aadha* | آدھا | Donkey | *gadha* | گدھا |

dh ڈھ = ھ + ڈ :-

| Drum | *dhōle* | ڈھول | Slope | *dhāl* | ڈھال |
| Loose | *dhilā* | ڈھیلا | Heap | *dhair* | ڈھیر |

th ٹھ = ھ + ٹ :-

| Cheat | *thag* | ٹھگ | Stick | *lathī* | لاٹھی |
| Wood | *kāth* | کاٹھ | To rise | *uthna* | اُٹھنا |

jh جھ = ھ + ج :-

| Swing | *jhula* | جھولا | Barren | *banjh* | بانجھ |
| Lake | *jheel* | جھیل | Cricket | *jhingur* | جھینگر |

39

kh ‍ کھ = ‍ہ + ک :-

Game	*khēl*	کھیل	Ash	*rākh*	راکھ
Fly	*makkhī*	مکھّی	Cucumber	*khirā*	کھیرا

gh ‍ گھ = ‍ہ + گ :-

Horse	*ghorā*	گھوڑا	House	*ghar*	گھر
Knee	*ghutna*	گھٹنا	Circle	*gherā*	گھیرا

DOUBLE LETTERS

The use of double letters is common in English, such as "mm" in "common". But such doubling of letters is rare in Urdu. You will come across only a few words with double letters.

Examples:

Cucumber	*kakrī*	ککڑی	Effort	*koshish*	کوشش
A small bird	*mamolā*	ممولا	Judge	*jaj*	جج
Uncle (Paternal)	*chachā*	چچا	Kid	*Nannah*	ننّھا

40

SILENT LETTERS

There are some Arabic words, common in Urdu, wherein a few letters are silent, *i.e.*, they are written but not pronounced.

Examples:

بالکل ; this word is written as *balkul*, but ا is silent, so it is read is *bilkul*, meaning 'quite'.

علی الصّباح ; this word is written as *ali-al-sabah*, but ل ۔ا۔ ی are silent, so it is read as *alassabah*, meaning 'early in the morning'.

There are many other such words which you will learn in due course.

Read and practise:

Boil	پھوڑا	Rice	بھات
Milk	دودھ	Knife	چھُری
Field	کھیت	Method	ڈھنگ
Slow	سُست	Watch	گھڑی
Straw	پھوس	Aunt	چچی
Group	جتھا	Responsibility	ذِمّہ
Lie	جھوٹ	Mistake	بھؤل

41

MEDIAL VOWEL-SIGNS

اَو	اُو	اَی	اِی	او	اِی	اُ	اِ	آ	ا
بَو	بُو	بَی	بِی	بو	بی	بُ	بِ	با	ب
چَو	چُو	چَی	چِی	چو	چی	چُ	چِ	چا	چ
دَو	دُو	دَی	دِی	دُو	دی	دُ	دِ	دا	د
سَو	سُو	سَی	سِی	سُو	سی	شُ	سِ	سا	س
طَو	طُو	طَیی	طِی	طُو	طی	طُ	طِ	طا	ط
کَو	کُو	کَی	کِی	کُ	کی	کِ		کا	ک
مَو	مُو	مَی	مِی	مُ	می	مُ	مِ	ما	م
لَو	لُو	لَی	لِی	لُ	لی	لُ	لِ	لا	ل

au	oo	ai	ee	o	e	u	i	aa	a
bau	boo	bai	bee	bo	be	bu	bi	baa	ba
chau	choo	chai	chae	cho	che	chu	chi	chaa	cha
dau	do	dai	de	doo	du	dee	di	daa	da
sau	so	sai	se	soo	su	see	si	saa	sa
tau	to	tai	te	too	tu	tee	ti	taa	ta
ku	ki	kai	kee	ke	kau	koo	ko	kaa	ka
mu	mi	mai	mee	me	mau	moo	mu	maa	ma
	lo	loo	lau	lo	lai	lee	li	laa	la

FINAL VOWEL-SIGNS

بی بے بَہ بوَ بوُں بوَ بوُ بو بہ بُ

سّے سے سی شُوں شُوَ شُوَ شہ شِ

دِئے وّے وے وی وں وو وہ و

لَائی لِئے لَا لے لی لوں لو لہ لُ لِ

گَائی گہ گئے گے گی گوں گا گ

وو لَائی پَو ہد اُو سے

bee	be	bbo	boon	bai	boo	bo	bah	ba
shshe	she	shee	shon	shoo	sho	shah	sha	
wi'e	wwe	we	wee	wan	wo	wah	wa	
llaa'ee	li'e	llaa	le	lee	lon	lo	lah	la
gaa'ee	gah	ga'e	ge	gee	gon	gao	ga	
	wah	llaa'ee	chau	mi	oo	she		

EXERCISE

کھیل

PLAY   l khe   **BAD**   raa bu

بُرا

مجھے

TO ME   jhe mu   **PROPER**   k thee

ٹھیک

پھول

FLOWER   l phoo   **GET UP**   th u

اُٹھ

43

	چَکّی		سَو
MILL-STONE	kee k cha	HUNDRED	u sa
	ہِمّت		کَوّا
COURAGE	t ma m hi	CROW	vaa v kau
	خَبر		بُھوک
NEWS	r ba kha	HUNGER	k bhoo
	نِڈر		مَرمّت
FEARLESS	r da ni	MENDING	t ma m ra ma
	ڈاک		وہاں
POST (Letter)	k daa	THERE	n haa wa
	محل		یہاں
PALACE	l ha ma	HERE	n haa ya
	دِین		ہاتھ
RELIGION	n dee	HAND	th haa
	بِنا		کِتاب
WITHOUT	naa bi	BOOK	b ta ki
	مِل		بھائی
MEET	l mi	BROTHER	ee bhaa
	اُڑ		نہیں
FLY	r u	NOT, NO	n hee na
	جُدا		گِیت
DIFFERENT	da ju	SONG	t gee

44

LESSON 6

GRAMMAR-I

NOUN

(Ism) إِسم

1. **Proper Nouns:** إِسم معرفہ (Ism Ma'rfa)

The following nouns come under this category:

(a) Names of persons:

احمد۔ رام۔ حامِد۔ عمر۔ کرشن۔ گاندھی۔ نہرو

(b) Names of places, countries etc.

دہلی۔ کلکتہ۔ مدراس۔ بھارت۔ ایران۔ امریکہ۔ جاپان

(c) Names of rivers, mountains etc.

گنگا۔ جمنا۔ سندھ۔ ہمالیہ۔ ایورسٹ۔ آلپس

Note: All proper nouns in Urdu are treated as such in English.

2. **Common Noun:** إِسم نکرہ (Ism Nakrah)

All nouns, except proper nouns, are regarded as common nouns. It will be useful to learn some of Urdu common nouns.

Example:

گھر۔ قلم۔ روٹی۔ خنجر۔ لڑکی۔ کتاب

45

PRONOUN

(Ism Zameer) اِسم ضمیر

I	*mai'n*	مَیں
THOU	*too*	تُو
HE, SHE, THAT	*wah*	وہ
WE	*ham*	ہم
YOU	*tum*	تُم
THEY	*wah*	وہ
WHO	*kaun*	گون
HE, SHE, THIS	*yah*	یہ
THEY (near)	*yah*	یہ
YOU (with respect)	*aap*	آپ
MY	*meraa*	میرا
YOUR	*tumhaaraa*	تُمہارا
OUR	*hamaaraa*	ہمارا

VERB

فعل *(Fail)*

A word used for saying something about a person or thing, indicating some action, is called a *verb*. Verbs are mainly of two kinds:

1. Intransitive   لازم   *(lazim).*

2. Transitive   متعدی   *(mutaddi).*

Intransitive Verb: A verb is intransitive if the action denoted by the verb stops with itself and it needs only the subject for completing the sense, *e.g.,*

میں بولا   (I said).

When an intransitive verb completes the sense with only a subject it is called فعل تام *(Fail Tám)*, a perfect verb as is the case in the above example میں بولا (I said) or احمد گیا (Ahmed went).

When a subject and an intransitive verb need something more to complete the sense the verb is called فعل ناقص *(Fa'il Naqis)*, an imperfect verb. For example: احمد تھا means nothing, but when we say احمد موجود تھا it means Ahmed was present.

In the sentence   احمد موجود تھا   Ahmed is subject, which is called مبتدا *(Mubtada)* and موجود is predicate which is called خبر *(khabar)* and تھا is an incomplete intransitive verb.

47

TRANSITIVE VERB
(Fa'il Mota'addi) فعل مُتعدّی

A verb is transitive, if the action or feeling denoted by the verb does not stop with itself, but is directed to some person or thing, that is, the verb requires an object in addition to the subject for completing the sense. For example:

اسلم نے کتاب پڑھی

In this example اسلم is subject فاعل (Fa'el), کتاب is object مفعول (Mafool) and پڑھی is a transitive verb.

Follwing are the فعل ناقص in Urdu.

I come. *(main ātā hūn)*	میں آتا ہوں۔
We come. *(ham āte hain)*	ہم آتے ہیں۔
Thou cometh. *(tū ātā hai)*	تو آتا ہے۔
You come. *(tum āte hō)*	تم آتے ہو۔
He comes. *(voh ātā hai)*	وہ آتا ہے۔
They come. *(voh log āte hain)*	وہ لوگ آتے ہیں۔
I will come. *(main āyūngā)*	میں آؤں گا۔
You will come. *(tum āo gē)*	تم آؤ گے۔
She will come. *(voh āyē gī)*	وہ آئے گی۔
I was coming. *(main ātā tha)*	میں آتا تھا۔
I was coming (for woman). *(main ati thi)*	میں آتی تھی۔
They were coming (for women). *(voh āti thin)*	وہ آتی تھیں۔

SOME VERBS

MAKE	banaa	بَنا
SPEAK	bol	بول
TAKE AWAY	le jaa	لے جا
KNOW	jaan	جان
CLEAN	saaf kar	صاف کر
WAIT, STAY	thahar	ٹھہر
MEET	mil	مِل
ASK	poochh	پُوچھ
TELL	bataa	بَتا
SEND	bhej	بھیج
DANCE	naach	ناچ
LIVE, REMAIN	rah	رہ
BE	ho	ہو
SLEEP	so	سو
PLAY	khel	کھیل
PUT	rakh	رکھ

LESSON 7

GRAMMAR - II

CASE

(Halate ism) حالتِ اسم

The most important are the Nominative and the Objective case.

(i) A Noun is said to be in the Nominative Case, when it is the name of something talked about, and when it is not governed by any Preposition; as: "The soldier drills". Here the "soldier" is in the Nominative Case because he does something.

(2) A Noun is said to be in the Objective Case, when something is done to it, or when it is governed by a Preposition or a Transitive Verb; as, "He sees the horse", "He was on the horse." In both sentences "horse" is in the Objective Case.

(3) In English no alteration is made in the actual spelling of a Noun when it is in the Objective case, but in Urdu alterations, in accordance with Rules given hereafter, are made in certain cases where it is governed by a Post-Position. All cases, except the Nominative Case, are called the Oblique Cases, which have different names according to the Post-Position following them.

Thus a Noun is said to be in the
Genitive Case if followed by "ka" – of
Dative   "   "   "   ko – to
Locative   "   "   "   par or meñ – at
Ablative   "   "   "   se – with
Agensive   "   "   "   ne – by
Vocative   "   "   "   ay! or O!

In the Accusative case the Noun is not governed by any Post-Position, because it is governed by a Transitive Verb; as: Kill a dog— *ek kuttā māro*.

Note: A Noun in the Accusative case has either the same form as a Nominative, as in English, or is expressed by "ko", like the Dative.

Oblique Singulars
(Singular Nouns followed by Post-Position)

1. Masculine Singular Nouns ending in "a" change the "a" into "e" before a Post-Position for the sake of euphony; as:

On the horse, *Ghoṛe par* گھوڑے پر (not *Ghora par*).

In the room, *Kamre men* کمرے میں (not *Kamra men*).

2. Masculine Singular Nouns not ending in "a" do not change.

3. Feminine Singular Nouns **never** change.

Oblique Plurals

The Oblique Plurals have but one rule, which is that all Plural Nouns (of whatever Gender or ending) have the suffix "on" when followed by a Post-Position. If, however, a Masculine Singular Noun ends in "a" the "a" is dropped before "on" for the sake of euphony; as:

Man	*admi*	– To the men	*ādmion ko*	آدمیوں کو
Table	*mēz*	– On the tables	*mēzon par*	میزوں پر
House	*ghar*	– In the houses	*gharon mēn*	گھروں میں
Office	*daftar*	– From the offices	*daftron sē*	دفتروں سے
Dog	*kuttā*	– To the dogs	*kutton ko*	کتوں کو
Cloth	*kaprā*	– On the clothes	*kapron par*	کپڑوں پر

51

Possessive Pronouns

My	Mera	میرا
Our	Hamāra	ہمارا
Your	Tumhāra	تمہارا
His/Her	Uskā	اُسکا

Adverbs

Here	Yahań	یہاں
There	Wahan	وہاں
O'clock	Baje	بجے
And (conj.)	Aur	اور
Yes	Hań	ہاں
No	Nahin	نہیں
Don't	Mat	مت
Now	Ab	اب

Observation

Possessive pronouns have the same position in Urdu as they have in English, *i.e.,* they must precede the Noun they govern.

The Adverb must be used just before the Verb: as:

Your knife is on the table (Your knife, table on, is)
— *Tumhàra chaqu mēz par hai.*

Bring that table here. (That table, here bring)
— *Woh mez yahàn lāo.*

Put this letter there. (This letter, there put)
— *Yeh chitthi wahān rakho.*

52

Come here at two o'clock. (Two o'clock, here come)
– *Do bajē yahàn aao.*

The servant is not in the house (Servant, house in, not is)
– *Naukar ghar mēn nahìn hai.*

EXERCISE

Translate into English:

Sanduq men	صندوق میں	*Sanduqon men*	صندوقوں میں
Ghar men	گھر میں	*Gharon men*	گھروں میں
Larkē ko	لڑکے کو	*Larkon ko*	لڑکوں کو
Ghore sē	گھوڑے سے	*Ghoron se*	گھوڑوں سے
Lifafe men	لفافے میں	*Lifafon men*	لفافوں میں
Ghori par	گھوڑی پر	*Ghorion par*	گھوڑیوں پر
Peti men	پیٹی میں	*Petiyon mēn*	پیٹیوں میں
Naukar ko	نوکر کو	*Naukaron ko*	نوکروں کو

Translate Into Urdu:

From the office	From the offices
In the window	In the windows
In the inkpot	In the inkpots
From the door	From the doors
To the mare	To the mares
On the horse	On the horses
To the dog	To the dogs
In the house	In the houses
In the box	In the boxes

THE ADJECTIVE

(Ism sifat) اسمِ صفت

An Adjective is a word joined to a Noun to show its quality (as, a strong man); size (as, a large book); colour (as, a red coat) or to describe it in any way.

Good	*Ach-chhā*	اچّھا	Bad	*Kharāb,* Burā	خراب، بُرا
True	*Sach-chā*	سچّا	False (Liar)	*Jhūtā*	جھوٹا
Hot	*Garm*	گرم	Cold	*Thandā*	ٹھنڈا
Dry	*Sūkhā*	سُوکھا	Wet	*Gilā*	گیلا
Clean, Clear	*Sāf*	صاف	Dirty	*Mailā*	میلا
Great, Large, Big	*Barā*	بڑا	Small, Little	*Chhotā*	چھوٹا
High	*Uñchā*	اُونچا	Low	*Nīchā*	نیچا
Long, Tall	*Lambā*	لمبا	Short	*Chhotā*	چھوٹا
Wide	*Chaurā*	چوڑا	Narrow	*Tañg*	تنگ
Deep	*Gahrā*	گہرا	Shallow	*Uthlā*	اُتھلا
All	*Sab*	سب	Few	*Chand*	چند
Dark	*Andhērā*	اندھیرا	Bright	*Raushan*	روشن
Young (youthful)	*Jawān*	جوان	Old (animate)	*Buddhā*	بڈھا
New	*Nayā*	نیا	Old (inanimate)	*Purānā*	پُرانا
Much	*Bahut*	بہت	A little (quantity)	*Thorā*	تھوڑا

54

1. If a Masculine Singular Noun is not followed by a Post-position, the final "a" of the Adjective does not change; as, a large dog— *ēk barā kuttā.*

2. If a Masculine Singular Noun is followed by a Post-position and before all Masculine Plural Nouns (whether followed by a Post-position or not) the final "a" of the Adjective is changed into "e"; as:

To the large dog.	*Barē kuttē ko.*	بڑے کُتّے کو
The large dogs.	*Barè kuttē.*	بڑے کُتّے
To the large dogs.	*Barē kuttoñ ko.*	بڑے کُتّوں کو

3. The final "a" of the Adjective is changed into "i" before all Feminine Nouns, whether Singular or Plural or whether followed by a Post-position or not; as:

A large mare.	*Barī ghorī.*	بڑی گھوڑی
On the large mare.	*Barī ghorī par.*	بڑی گھوڑی پر
On the large mares.	*Barī ghorioñ par.*	بڑی گھوڑیوں پر

Some Adjectives

Rich	*Ameer*	امیر
Poor	*Ghareeb*	غریب
Easy	*Āasaan*	آسان
Difficult	*Mushkil*	مشکل
Well	*Tan-durust*	تندرست
Ill	*Bīmār*	بیمار
Wise	*Aqlmand*	عقلمند
Foolish	*Bēwaqūf*	بیوقوف
Hard	*Sakht*	سخت

55

Swift (speedy)	*Tēz*	تیز
Slow	*Dhīmā or halkā*	دھیما، ہلکا
Sharp (fine-edged)	*Tēz*	تیز
Blunt	*Kund*	کُند
Active	*Chust*	چُست
Lazy	*Sust*	سُست
Beautiful	*Khūbsūrat*	خوبصورت
Ugly	*Badsūrat*	بدصورت
Soft	*Narm*	نرم
Honest	*Imāndār*	ایماندار
Dishonest	*Bē-īmān*	بےایمان
Strong	*Mazboot*	مضبوط
Weak	*Kamzor*	کمزور
Dear (expensive)	*Mahñgā*	مہنگا
Cheap	*Sastā*	ستا

The Interrogative and Relative Pronouns etc.

1. When asking a question, if there is no word (such as "why", "what", etc.). which shows that the sentence is interrogative, either use the word "kiā" (what) at the beginning or simply raise the voice at the end.

Is that your horse?

Kiā woh tumhārā ghorā haī ? کیا وہ تمہارا گھوڑا ہے؟

Is my book on the table?

Kia mērī kitāb mēz par hai ? کیا میری کتاب میز پر ہے؟

THE ADVERBS

(Mutaeleq fail) متعلق فعل

The Adverbs are of several kinds, most of which are given below under different headings.

Now	Ab	اب
Always	Hamēsha	ہمیشہ
Just now	Abhī	ابھی
Quickly	Jaldī sē	جلدی سے
Yet	Abhī tak	ابھی تک
Soon	Jaldī	جلدی
Again, then	Phir	پھر
Ever	Kabhī	کبھی
In future	Āainda	آئندہ
Never	Kabhī nahīn	کبھی نہیں
Every day	Har roz	ہر روز
Suddenly	Achānak	اچانک
Now-a-days	Āaj kal	آج کل
Now and then/ Sometimes	Kabhī kabhī	کبھی کبھی
Often	Aksar	اکثر
At present	Filhāl	فی الحال
In turns	Bārī bārī	باری باری

57

Adverbs of Place

Everywhere	*Har jagah*	ہر جگہ
Nowhere	*Kahīñ nahīñ*	کہیں نہیں
By sea	*Sumandar kē rāstē*	سمندر کے راستے
By land	*Khushkī kē rāstē*	خشکی کے راستے
By air	*Hawāī jahāz sē*	ہوائی جہاز سے

Adverbs of Quantity

A little	*Thorā*	تھوڑا	Alone	*Akēlā*	اکیلا
Even	*Bhī*	بھی	Enough	*Kaafī*	کافی
Only	*Sirf*	صرف	Some	*Kuchh*	کچھ

Adverbs of Affirmation

| Yes | *Hañ* | ہاں | Undoubtedly/ | | |
| Certainly | *Zarūr* | ضرور | Indeed | *Bē shak* | بے شک |

Adverbs of Negation

| No, Not | *Nahin* | نہیں | Otherwise | *Warna/* | ورنہ/ |
| Not at all | *Bilkul nahin* | بالکل نہیں | | *nahīñ to* | نہیں تو |

58

Arabic Adverbs
Commonly Used in Urdu

At once	Fauran	فوراً
About (nearly)	Taqriban	تقریباً
Per force	Majburan	مجبوراً
By force	Jabran	جبراً
For example	Masalan	مثلاً
By chance	Ittifāqan	اتفاقاً
Probably	Ghāliban	غالباً
Especially	Khusūsan	خصوصاً
Commonly/ Usually	Umūman	عموماً
Approximately	Takhmīnan	تخميناً
Surely	Yaqīnan	يقيناً

THE CONJUNCTION

(Harf ataf) حرف عطف

A conjunction is a word, which is used to connect two words or sentences; as:

| And | Aur | اور | That | Keh | کہ |
| Or | Yā | یا | If | Agar | اگر |

59

But	Lēkin	لیکن	Also, even	Bhī	بھی
However	Magar	مگر	Yet (even then)	Phir bhī	پھر بھی
Because	Kionkeh	کیونکہ	Although	Agarcheh	اگر چہ
Since	Chūñkeh	چونکہ	Therefore	Is līē	اس لئے
According	Chunāñcheh	چنانچہ	Likewise	Is hī tarah	اس ہی طرح

THE INTERJECTION

حرف فجا (Harf fija)

O! "O" or "Ai"	اوے	Hurrah	Wāh Wāh	واہ واہ
Well done Bravo	Shābāsh شاباش	Is it really?	Kiā such much	کیا سچ مچ
Eh! what!	Haiñ ہیں	Be careful	Khabardār	خبردار

THE VERB

فعل (Fail)

There are two principal kinds of Verbs, *viz.,* Transitive and Intransitive.

(a) A verb is Transitive, if the action has an object without which the sense would be incomplete; as:

60

(a) The dog killed a fox. I saw a man.

Here the sense would be incomplete without mentioning "fox" and "man" and therefore the Verbs "kill" and "see" are both Transitive.

(b) A Verb is Intransitive if the action does not pass to an Object; as:

The servant is sleeping. Thy boy ran.

Here the sense is already complete without placing any objects after the Verbs "sleep" or "run". They are therefore Intransitive.

Note: *The Transitive and Intransitive Verbs differ in their use only in the Past Tense.*

THE INFINITIVE

(Masder) مصدر

The Infinitive expresses only the action or state and is not limited as regards person, number and time; as,

To come, To cut, To fall, To write, etc.

As in English every Infinitive is preceded by "To" so in the same way every Infinitive in Urdu terminates in "na",

EXAMPLES

Intransitives			Transitives		
To come	*Ānā*	آنا	To see	*Dēkhnā*	دیکھنا
To go	*Jānā*	جانا	To show	*Dikhānā*	دکھانا
To take away To carry }	*Lejānā*	لیجانا	To say To tell }	*Kahnā*	کہنا

61

To sleep	Sonā	سونا	To eat	Khānā	کھانا
To fall	Girnā	گرنا	To give	Dēnā	دینا
To walk	Chalnā	چلنا	To send	Bhējnā	بھیجنا
To wake (oneself)	Jāgnā	جاگنا	To drop	Girānā	گرانا
			To awaken	jagānā	جگانا
To speak	Bolnā	بولنا	To call	Bulānā	بلانا
To lie down	Lēṭnā	لیٹنا	To change	Badalnā	بدلنا
To laugh	Hañsnā	ہنسنا	To write	Likhnā	لکھنا
To bring	Laanā	لانا	To drink	Pīnā	پینا
To sit	Baiṭhnā	بیٹھنا	To open	Kholnā	کھولنا
To wait	Thaherṅā	ٹھہرنا	To shut	Band kārnā	بند کرنا
To rise	Uṭhnā	اُٹھنا	To raise		
To arrive			To lift up	Uṭhānā	اُٹھانا
To reach	Pahuñchna	پہنچنا	To pick up		
To climb			To keep		
To mount	Charhnā	چڑھنا	To put	Rakhnā	رکھنا
To get on			To place		

THE IMPERATIVE

(Amar) امر

The Urdu Verbs are quite simple and regular in form and it wants but little practice to form any particular part or tense of a Verb, if we know the Infinitive of it.

(a) The root of a Verb is obtained by omitting the final

"na" of the Infinitive; as,

To go	*Jānā*	جانا	Root	*Jā*	جا
To speak	*Bolnā*	بول	Root	*Bol*	بول

(b) The Imperative or "word of command" is formed by adding "o" to the root of a Verb' as:

Verbs		Root	Imperative	
To speak	*Bolnā*	*Bol*	*Bolo*	بولو
To strike	*Mārnā*	*Mār*	*Māro*	مارو
To drop	*Girānā*	*Girā*	*Girāo*	گراؤ

Note: If the root ends either in "e" or "o", these vowels are dropped, for the sake of euphony, before the termination "o" of the Imperative; as:

Verbs		Root	Imperative
To give	*Dēnā*	*Dē*	*Do*
To sleep	*Sonā*	*So*	*So*

EXAMPLES

1. Come into the room.

کمرہ میں آؤ۔

   Kamrē me aao.

2. Bring my horse.

میرا گھوڑا لاؤ۔

   Mērā ghorā lāo.

3. Take all things away.

سب چیزیں لیجاؤ۔

   Sab chīzēn lējāo.

4. Open that box.

وہ صندوق کھولو۔

   Woh sandūq kholo.

63

5. Put that paper in my pocket. وہ کاغذ میری جیب میں رکھو۔

    Woh kāghaz mērī jēb mēñ rakho.

6. Send this letter to the shop. یہ خط دوکان کو بھیجو۔

    Yeh khat dukan ko bhējo.

Prohibition is expressed by using the particle "mat" — "do not" or "don't" before the Imperative; as:

1. Do not (or don't) go to the office today.

    Aaj daftar ko mat jāo. آج دفتر کو مت جاؤ۔

2. Don't sit on the chair.

    Kursī par mat baitho. کرسی پر مت بیٹھو۔

THE PREPOSITION "to"

(Harf jaar) حرف جار

The preposition "to" must be translated by "ke pas" (and not by "ko") when it is used before a human being (or a Pronoun), with any of the following Verbs, (which it will be noticed, involve movement from one place to another):

To go	*Jānā*	جانا	To bring	*Lānā*	لانا
To come	*Aanā*	آنا	To take to	*Lējānā*	لیجانا
To send	*Bhējnā*	بھیجنا	To reach	*Pahuñchnā*	پہنچنا

Note: Before inanimate objects "to" take its ordinary form "ko".

EXAMPLES

Go to the Post Master. پوسٹ ماسٹر صاحب کے پاس جاؤ۔

Post Master sāheb kē pās jāo.

Go to the Post Office. ڈاک خانہ کو جاؤ۔

Dāk khāne ko jāo.

Take this letter to my son. یہ خط میرے بیٹے کے پاس لیجاؤ۔

Yeh khat mērē bētē kē pās lējāo.

Come to me tomorrow morning. کل صبح میرے پاس آؤ۔

Kal subah mērē pās aao.

Infinitives

Intransitives			Transitives		
To run	*Daurnā*	دوڑنا	To hear	*Sunnā*	سُننا
To die	*Marnā*	مرنا	To know	*Jaannā*	جاننا
To flow	*Bahnā*	بہنا	To cut	*Kaatnā*	کاٹنا
To come out	*Nikalnā*	نکلنا	To take out	*Nikaalnà*	نکالنا
To fly	*Uṛnā*	اُڑنا	To fill	*Bharnā*	بھرنا
To be angry	*Khafā honā*	خفا ہونا	To under- stand	*Samajhnā*	سمجھنا
To live	*Rahnā*	رہنا	To do	*Karnā*	کرنا

65

To smile	*Muskuraanā*	مُسکرانا		To work	*Kaam karnā*	کام کرنا
To burn	*Jalnā*	جَلنا		To take	*Lēnā*	لینا
To escape (from punishment etc.)	*Bachnā*	بچنا		To throw	*Phēñknā*	پھینکنا
				To make	*Banaanā*	بنانا
To escape (from danger etc.)	*Bhaagnā*	بھاگنا		To read	*Paṛhnā*	پڑھنا
				To ask	*Pūchhnā*	پوچھنا
To be / To have	*Honā*	ہونا		To burn / To light	*Jalaanā*	جلانا
To advance / To come forward	*Aage baṛhnā*	آگے بڑھنا		To sell	*Bēchnā*	بیچنا
				To buy	*Kharidnā/ Mol lēnā*	خریدنا/ مول لینا
To become	*Hojana*	ہوجانا		To clean	*Sāf karnā*	صاف کرنا
To retreat/ To get back	*Pichhè haṭnā*	پیچھے ہٹنا		To strike / To hit / To beat	*Maarnā*	مارنا
To weep / To cry	*Ronā*	رونا		To kill	*Mārdālnā*	مارڈالنا
To shout / To cry / To scream	*Chillaanā*	چِلّانا		To prepare / To get ready	*Taiyār karnā*	تیار کرنا
				To steal	*Churana*	چُرانا
To swim	*Tairnā*	تیرنا		To break	*Tornà*	توڑنا
To get down / To dismount	*Utarnā*	اترنا		To take off	*Utaarnā*	اُتارنا
				To put on	*Pahennā*	پہننا
				To teach	*Sikhaanā*	سکھانا

CONJUGATIONS

(Gardaan) گردان

Present Indicative (or Indefinite)

Singular

I go.	*Maiñ jaata huñ*	میں جاتا ہوں۔
Thou goest.	*Tū jaatā hai.*	تو جاتا ہے۔
He goes.	*Woh jaatā hai.*	وہ جاتا ہے۔
She goes.	*Woh jaatī hai.*	وہ جاتی ہے۔

Plural

We go.	*Ham jaatē haiñ.*	ہم جاتے ہیں۔
You go.	*Tum jaatē ho.*	تم جاتے ہو۔
They go.	*Woh jaatē haiñ.*	وہ جاتے ہیں۔
They go (fem.)	*Woh jaatī haiñ.*	وہ جاتی ہیں۔

Present Continuous (or Definite)

Singular

I am going.	*Maiñ jā rahā hūñ.*	میں جا رہا ہوں۔
Thou art going.	*Tu jā raha hai.*	تو جا رہا ہے۔
He is going.	*Woh jā rahā hai.*	وہ جا رہا ہے۔
She is going.	*Woh jā rahī hai.*	وہ جا رہی ہے۔

Plural

We are going.	*Ham jā rahē haiñ.*	ہم جا رہے ہیں۔
You are going.	*Tum jà rahe ho.*	تم جا رہے ہو۔
They are going.	*Woh jā rahē haiñ.*	وہ جا رہے ہیں۔
They are going (fem.)	*Woh jā rahī haiñ*	وہ جا رہی ہیں۔

Substantives used as Postpositions

Near	kē qaríb, or	کے قریب /
	kē nazdik, or	کے نزدیک /
	kē paas	کے پاس
on account of	kē sabab	کے سبب
Under, below	kē níche	کے نیچے
Behind	kē píchhe	کے پیچھے
For	kē waastē or kē líē	کے واسطے / کے لئے
Without	kē baghair	کے بغیر
With	kē saath	کے ساتھ
In the middle of	ke bich mēñ	کے بیچ میں
Between	kē darmiān	کے درمیان
Instead of	ke bādlē	کے بدلے
Beyond	kē parē	کے پرے
According to	kē muāfiq	کے موافق
Round	ke gird	کے گرد
Round about	kē aas paas	کے آس پاس
In front of	ke saamnē	کے سامنے
Before (ahead)	kē aagē	کے آگے
Before (in time)	sē pahlē	سے پہلے
After (in time)	ke bād	کے بعد
Inside	kē andar	کے اندر
Outside	kē baaher	کے باہر
Against	ke khilaaf	کے خلاف

68

POSTPOSITIONS
(Haruf-e-Jaar) حروفِ جار

A Preposition is called a Postposition in Urdu. It is used after the Noun or Pronoun.

Example:-

Pronoun		Noun		Postposition	
To him	اُس کو	To Nazeer	نذیر کو	to	کو
From him	اُس سے	From house	گھر سے	from	سے
Of his	اُس کا	Of house	گھر کا	of	کا
In him	اُس میں	In house	گھر میں	in	میں
On him	اُس پر	On house	گھر پر	on	پر
Upto him	اُس تک	Upto house	گھر تک	upto	تک

Read these sentences taking care on Postpositions.

See this man.	اِس آدمی کو دیکھو۔
Write with the pen.	قلم سے لِکھو۔
Give money to Nazeer.	نذیر کو روپیہ دو۔
This woman's son.	اِس عَورت کا بیٹا۔
It is his house.	یہ اُس کا گھر ہے۔
Come upto the shop.	دُوکان تک آؤ۔
Picture is on the wall.	دِیوار پر تصویر ہے۔

69

OBLIQUE-SINGULAR

تِرچھا واحد *(Tirchha Wahed)*

See him.	اُسے دیکھو۔
Stay at home.	گھر پر رہو۔
Meet Roshan Ara.	روشن آرا سے ملو۔
Call that beggar.	اُس فقیر کو بُلا وَ۔
Give to Raheem.	رحیم کو دو۔
He is in the bath-room.	وہ غُسل خانہ میں ہے۔
Bring from that small room.	اُس چھوٹے کمرے سے لاؤ۔
It is of my elder son.	یہ میرے بڑے لڑکے کا ہے۔
I stay in this big room.	مَیں اِس بڑے کمرے میں رہتا ہوں۔

A Noun or Pronoun, when used without a Postposition, is in the Nominative Case, while the Oblique Case is always governed by a Postposition, e.g.,

Oblique			**Nominative**		
At home	=	گھر پر	Home	=	گھر
To the man	=	آدمی کو	man	=	آدمی

2. In Oblique Case, Masculine Nouns, Pronouns and Adjectives ending in "aa" change the final 'aa' into 'e' for the singular, e.g., میرے بڑے لڑکے کا

70

OBLIQUE - PLURAL

(Tirchha Jamaa) تِرچھا جمع

At homes	گھروں میں۔
Of boys	لڑکوں کا۔
Give to poors.	غریبوں کو دو۔
Open those windows.	اُن کھڑکیوں کو کھولو۔
Call those students.	اُن طالِب علموں کو بُلاؤ۔
These are the matters of women.	یہ عورتوں کی باتیں ہیں۔
Buy my black horses.	میرے کالے گھوڑوں کو خرید لو۔

Who is better among those new servants.

اُن نئے نوکروں میں کون بہتر ہے۔

Leave those old matters.

اُن پُرانی باتوں کو چھوڑ دو۔

1. The Oblique Plural is formed by adding *'oun'* to all the Masculine and Feminine Nouns.

Plural		**Singular**	
At houses =	گھروں میں	At house =	گھر میں
Of women =	عورتوں کی	Of woman =	عورت کی

2. Masculine Nouns ending in *'aa'* drop the *'aa'* before the *'oun'* is added.

To boys = لڑکوں کو ; To boy = لڑکے کو ; boy = لڑکا

3. Adjectives and Pronouns do not change for Oblique Plural. They remain in the ordinary inflected form.

To my elder son. = میرے بڑے لڑکے کو۔

71

PERSONAL PRONOUN

(Zameer kee qisme'n) ضمیر کی قسمیں

I am here.	میں یہاں ہوں۔
He is there.	وہ اُدھر ہے۔
We are at home.	ہم گھر پر ہیں۔
Give my book.	میری کتاب دو۔
What is his name?	اس کا نام کیا ہے۔
He is my son.	یہ میرا بیٹا ہے۔
Where is your boy?	تمہارا لڑکا کہاں ہے؟
Give me a book.	مجھے ایک کتاب دو۔
Don't fall on him.	اس پر مَت گرو۔
Give that letter to me.	وہ خط مجھ کو دو۔
Bring it from him.	اس سے یہ لے آؤ۔
Come upto us.	ہمارے پاس آؤ۔
Take pity on me.	مجھ پر رحم کرو۔
Come to our house.	ہمارے گھر آئیے۔

POSSESSIVE PRONOUN

(Zameer ke saath izaafah) ضمیر کے ساتھ اضافہ

She is my mother.	یہ میری ماں ہے۔
What is your name?	تمہارا نام کیا ہے؟
My father is not here.	میرے والد یہاں نہیں ہیں۔
It is his village.	یہ اس کا گاؤں ہے۔
India is our home-land.	بھارت ہمارا وطن ہے۔
Bring my book.	میری کتاب لاؤ۔
Is he your friend?	کیا وہ تمہارا دوست ہے؟
Give the rent of my house today.	آج میرے گھر کا کرایہ دے دو۔
The price of his pen is much.	اس کے قلم کا دام زیادہ ہے۔
All these are his.	یہ سب اُس کے ہیں۔
Today we will get our ration.	ہماری رسد آج ملے گی۔

First and Second Person Singular and Plural take *'raa'* and *'ree'* in the place of *'kaa'*, *'ke'* and *'kee'*.

میں + کا ← میں+را ← میرا، میرے، میری
ہم + کا ← ہم+را ← ہمارا، ہمارے، ہماری
تو + کا ← تو+را ← تیرا، تیرے، تیری
تم + کا ← تم+را ← تمہارا، تمہارے، تمہاری

POSSESSIVE CASE

اضافی (Izaafi)

He is his son.	یہ اس کا لڑکا ہے۔
It is this man's house.	یہ اس آدمی کا گھر ہے۔
She is that man's daughter.	یہ اس آدمی کی لڑکی ہے۔
They are his sons.	وہ اس کے لڑکے ہیں۔
It is your will.	یہ آپ کی مرضی ہے۔
Yaqub's wedding is tomorrow.	یعقوب کی شادی کل ہے۔
Bring from that shop.	اس دوکان سے لاؤ۔
I come from Nina's house.	نینا کے گھر سے آتی ہوں۔
Give the answer of this letter.	اس خط کا جواب دو۔

1. The Postposition of Possessive Case is *'kaa'* which agrees with the thing possessed in Gender and Number, for example;

رحیم کی گھوڑی   رحیم کا گھوڑا

رحیم کی گھوڑیاں   رحیم کے گھوڑے

2. The *'kaa'*. 'کا' becomes *'ke'* کے before the Oblique.

رحیم کے گھوڑے پر

رحیم کے گھوڑوں پر

LESSON 8
GENDER
(Jins) جنس

The Urdu language has only two Genders, *i.e.*, the Masculine Gender and the Feminine Gender and no Neuter Gender.

Males are called *Masculine* and Females *Feminine*.

(1) Nouns that end in "a", with very few exceptions, are Masculines: as, *Larkā* — a boy; *Kaprā* — cloth.

(2) Nouns that end in "i" are almost always Feminine; as, *Larkī* — a girl; *Gārī* — a carriage. *Ādmī* (man) or *bhai* (brother) are masculines by meaning.

Masculines

(Muzakkar) مُذَکّر

Boy	*Larkā*	لڑکا
Son	*Bētā*	بیٹا
Horse	*Ghorā*	گھوڑا
Dog	*Kuttā*	کُتّا
Room	*Kamra*	کمرہ
Door	*Darwāza*	دروازہ
Cloth	*Kaprā*	کپڑا
Egg	*Andā*	انڈا

75

Envelope	Lifāfa	لفافہ
Lock	Tālā	تالا
Hour, Clock	Ghanta	گھنٹہ
Bathroom	Ghusl Khana	غسل خانہ
Brother	Bhāi	بھائی
Husband	Khawind	خاوند

Feminines
(Moennas) مونث

Girl	Larki	لڑکی
Daughter	Beti	بیٹی
Mare	Ghori	گھوڑی
Bitch	Kutyā	کتیا
Window	Khirki	کھڑکی
Key	Chābi	چابی
Watch	Ghari	گھڑی
Carriage	Gāri	گاڑی
Turban	Pagri	پگڑی
Ink	Roushnai	روشنائی
Saddle	Zeen	زین
Inkpot	Dawat	دوات
Sister	Bahen	بہن
Wife	Biwi	بیوی

LESSON 9

GROUP OF TERMS

TIME

وقت (Waqt)

WATCH	gharee	گھڑی
O'CLOCK	baje	بجے
HOUR	ghantah	گھنٹہ
MORNING	subha	صبح
NOON	do pahar	دوپہر
EVENING	shaam	شام
NIGHT	raat	رات
MIDNIGHT	aadhi raat	آدھی رات
DAY	din	دن
WEEK	haftah	ہفتہ
FORTNIGHT	do hafte	دو ہفتے
MONTH	maheenah	مہینہ
YEAR	saal, baras	سال، برس
CENTURY	sadee	صدی
WEEKLY	haftahwar	ہفتہ وار
MONTHLY	mahaana	ماہانہ
YEARLY	salana	سالانہ
YESTERDAY	kal (guzishtah)	کل (گزشتہ)
TOMORROW	kal (Aaiendah)	کل (آئندہ)
TODAY	aaj	آج
NOW-A-DAYS	Aajkal	آج کل

Afternoon	*Tisre pahar*	تیسرے پہر
At sun-rise	*Din nikle*	دن نکلے
At sun-set	*Din chhupe*	دن چھپے
Every	*Har Ek*	ہر ایک
Once	*Ek dafa*	ایک دفعہ
Twice	*Do dafa*	دو دفعہ
This morning	*Aaj subah ko*	آج صبح کو
This evening	*Aaj sham ko*	آج شام کو
To-night	*Aaj rat ko*	آج رات کو
Last week	*Pichhle hafte*	پچھلے ہفتہ
Next week	*Agle hafte*	اگلے ہفتہ
Early	*Sawere*	سویرے

WEEK
(Haftah) ہفتہ

SUNDAY	*Itwar*	اِتوار
MONDAY	*peer*	پیر
TUESDAY	*mangal*	منگل
WEDNESDAY	*budh*	بدھ
THURSDAY	*jumeraat*	جمعرات
FRIDAY	*jumaah*	جمعہ
SATURDAY	*sanichar*	سنیچر
WEEK	*haftah*	ہفتہ
WEEKLY	*haftawaar*	ہفتہ وار
DAY (24 hours)	*rouz*	روز
DAY (12 hours)	*din*	دِن
DAILY	*har rouz*	ہر روز

78

MONTHS

(Maheene) مہینے

JAN	*janwaree*	جنوری	muharram	مُحَرّم
FEB	*farwaree*	فروری	safar	صَفَر
MAR	*maarch*	مارچ	rabbeeu'l awwal	رَبِیعُ الاوّل
APR	*aprel*	اپریل	rabbeeu'l aakhir	رَبِیعُ الآخِر
MAY	*ma'ee*	مئی	jamaadeeu'l awwal	جَمادِی الاوّل
JUN	*joon*	جُون	jamaadeeu'l aakhir	جَمادِی الآخِر
JUL	*joolaa'ee*	جُولائی	rajjab	رَجَب
AUG	*agast*	اگست	shaaban	شَعبَان
SEP	*sitambar*	ستمبر	ramzaan	رَمَضان
OCT	*aktobar*	اکتوبر	shawwaal	شَوَّال
NOV	*nawambar*	نُومبر	ziqaedah	ذِیقَعده
DEC	*disambar*	دِسمبر	zeelhajjah	ذِی الحِجّہ

NATURE

Mazahire Fitrat مظاہر فطرت

SUN	sooraj	سُورج
MOON	chaand	چاند
MOONLIGHT	chaandnee	چاندنی
SUNSHINE	dhoop	دُھوپ
STAR	sitaarah	سِتارہ
WORLD	dunyaa	دُنیا
SKY	aasmaan	آسمان
OCEAN	samandar	سَمندر
RIVER	daryaa	دَریا
MOUNTAIN	pahaaṛ	پہاڑ
WIND (air)	hawaa	ہَوا
FIRE	aag	آگ
THUNDER	garaj	گرج
RAINBOW	Qouso Qizah	قوس وقزح

80

SEASON & CLIMATE

(Mausam wa aab-o-hawaa) مَوسم و آب و ہَوا

SPRING	bahaar	بہار
SUMMER	garmi	گرمی
RAINY SEASON	barsaat	برسات
WINTER	jaara	جاڑا
COLD	thanda	ٹھنڈا
HEAT WARMTH	garamee	گرمی
WARM	garam	گرم
FROST	paala	پالا
FOGGY	dhundlaa	دُھندلا
RAIN	baarish	بارِش
FOG	kuhraa	کُہرا
CLOUDY	badlee	بَدلی
STORM	toofaan	طُوفان
SUNSHINE	dhoop	دُھوپ

DIRECTION

(Simt) سمت

NORTH	shumaal	شُمال
SOUTH	janoob	جُنوب
EAST	mashriq	مَشرِق
WEST	maghrib	مَغرِب
LEFT SIDE	baayee'n taraf	بائیں طرف
RIGHT SIDE	daayee'n taraf	دائیں طرف
RIGHT	daayaa'n	دایاں
LEFT	baayaa'n	بایاں
ONWARD	aage	آگے
BACKWARD	peeche	پیچھے
ABOVE	oopar	اُوپر
BELOW	neeche	نیچے
BEYOND	ustaraf	اُس طرف
INSIDE	andar	اَندر
OUTSIDE	baahar	باہر

PARTS OF THE BODY

(Aadhaae Jism) اعضائے جسم

BONE	haddi	ہڈّی
SKIN	khaal	کھال
BLOOD	khoon	خُون
BRAIN	dimaagh	دِماغ
LIVER	jigar	جِگر
HAND	haath	ہاتھ
CLAW	panjaa	پنجا
FINGER	ungalee	اُنگلی
NAIL	naakhun	ناخُن
BEARD	daarhee	داڑھی
NECK	gardan	گردن
EYEBROW	abru	اُبرو
CHEEK	gaal	گال
EYE LASH	palak	پلک
LEG	taañg	ٹانگ
ARM	bāzu	بازو
NOSE	naak	ناک
EYE	aañkh	آنکھ

FAMILY

(Khandaan) خاندان

MOTHER	*maa'n, waalida*	ماں،والِدہ
FATHER	*abbaa, waalid*	اَبّا،والِد
SON	*betaa*	بیٹا
DAUGHTER	*betee*	بیٹی
BROTHER	*bhaa'ee*	بھائی
SISTER	*bahan*	بہن
FOSTER	*sautelaa*	سَوتیلا
COUSIN	*rishte ka bhaa'ee*	رشتہ کابھائی
BOY	*larkaa*	لڑکا
GIRL	*larkee*	لڑکی
CHILD	*bachchah*	بچّہ
PARENTS	*waalidain*	والِدین
HUSBAND	*shauhar*	شَوہر
WIFE	*beewee*	بیوی

84

MAN	aadmee	آدمی
WOMAN	aurat	عَورت
NEPHEW	bhateejaa	بھتیجا
UNCLE (Paternal)	chachaa	چچا
UNCLE (Maternal)	maamoo'n	مامُوں
AUNT (Maternal)	<u>kh</u>aalah	خالہ
AUNT (Paternal)	phoophee	پھُوپھی
GRANDFATHER	daadaa	دادا
BROTHER-IN-LAW	saalaa	سالا، برادرنسبتی
FATHER-IN-LAW	sasur	سَسُر
MOTHER-IN-LAW	saas	ساس
SON-IN-LAW	daamaad	داماد
DAUGHTER-IN-LAW	bahoo	بَہُو
GUARDIAN	sarparast	سرپرست
ANCESTOR	aabaw ajdad	آباوَاجداد
RELATIVE	rishtedaar	رِشتہ دار

MARRIAGE

(Shaadee) شادی

ENGLISH	Transliteration	Urdu
BRIDE	dulhan	دُلہن
BRIDEGROOM	dulhaa	دُلہا
FLOWER	phool	پھُول
CEREMONY	taqreeb	تقریب
INVITATION	da'wat	دعوت
GARLAND	haar	ہار
JEWELS	jawaahir	جواہر
ORNAMENT	zewar	زیور
PERFUME	khushboo	خُوشبُو
PEARL	motee	موتی
RING	angoothi	انگُوٹھی
SONG	geet	گِیت
BAND	baajaa	باجا
DIVORCE	ṭallaq	طلّاق

DRESS AND GARMENTS

(Kapre wa poshaak)   کپڑے و پوشاک

ROBE	libaas	لِباس
RIBBON	feetah	فیتہ
TOWEL	tauliyah	تولیہ
SHIRT	qamees	قمیص
TROUSER	paaijaamah	پائجامہ
BODICE	angiyaa	اَنگِیا
NAPKIN	anguchhaa	اَنگوچھا
COAT	cot	کوٹ
HALF PANT	naiker	نیکر
SHAWL	dushaalaa	دوشالا
TURBAN	pagree	پگڑی
SARI	saaree	ساڑی
GLOVE	dastaanah	دستانہ
SOCKS	mozah	موزہ

HAT, CAP	topee	ٹوپی
HANDKERCHIEF	rumaal	رُومال
BELT	peṭee	پیٹی
WOOLLEN	oonee	اُونی
VELVET	makhmal	مخمل
SILK	resham	ریشم
BLANKET	kambal	کمبل
PILLOW	takyah	تکیہ
CUSHION	gaddee	گدّی
CURTAIN	pardah	پردہ
TABLECLOTH	mezposh	میزپوش
SHEET	chaadar	چادر
BEDDING	bichhaunaa	بچھونا
BORDER	kinaaraa	کِنارا
PETTI-COAT	lahangaa	لہنگا
MUFFLER	gulooband	گُلوبند

ANIMALS

(Jaanwar) جانوَر

COW	gaa'e	گائے
DOG	kuttaa	کُتّا
GOAT	bakree	بکری
CAMEL	oonṭ	اُونٹ
DONKEY	gadhaa	گدھا
MONKEY	bandar	بندر
BEAST	haiwaan	حَیوان
BUFFALO	bhains	بھینس
BULLOCK	bail	بیل
CALF	bachhraa	بچھڑا
CATTLE	maweshee	مَویشی
DEER	hiran	ہرن
ELEPHANT	haathee	ہاتھی
FOX	lomṛee	لومڑی

89

JACKAL	geedar	گِیدڑ
WOLF	bheriyaa	بھیڑیا
LION	sher babar	شیر ببر
TIGER	sher	شیر
PANTHER	cheetaa	چیتا
HORSE	ghoraa	گھوڑا
HARE	khargosh	خرگوش
LIZARD	chhipkalee	چھپکلی
MOUSE	choohaa	چُوہا
CROCODILE	magar machh	مگرمچھ
CAT	billee	بِلّی
LAMB	memnaa	میمنا
HOUND	shikaaree kuttaa	شِکاری کُتّا
PIG	suwwar	سُوّر
FROG	mendak	مینڈک
MONKEY	bandar	بندر

90

BIRDS

(Parinday) پرندے

English	Transliteration	Urdu
CROW	kawwa	کوّا
COCK	murgha	مُرغا
DUCK	batakh	بطخ
DOVE	faakhtah	فاختہ
PIGEON	kabootar	کبوتر
PARROT	totaa	طوطا
SPARROW	chiryaa	چڑیا
KITE	cheel	چیل
OWL	ullu	اُلّو
PARTRIDGE	teetar	تیتر
PEACOCK	mor	مور
BAT	chimgaadar	چمگادڑ
BUTTERFLY	titlee	تِتلی
NIGHTINGALE	bulbul	بُلبُل

91

DOMESTIC ARTICLES

(Gharailu cheezen) گھریلوچیزیں

PLATE	rakaabee	رکابی
CUP	piyalah	پیالہ
BASIN	bartan	برتن
BUCKET	baaltee	بالٹی
KNIFE	chhuree	چھری
PENKNIFE	chaaqoo	چاقو
SPOON	chamchah	چمچہ
FORK	kaantaa	کانٹا
SAUCER	pirch	پرچ
BROOM	jhaaroo	جھاڑو
MATCH	diyaa salaa'ee	دِیاسلائی
LOCK	taalaa	تالا
KEY	chaabee	چابی
BOTTLE	botal	بوتل

PICTURE	tasweer	تصویر
BASKET	tokree	ٹوکری
MIRROR	ainah	آئینہ
CANDLE	mombattee	موم بتّی
TABLE	mez	میز
CHAIR	kursee	کُرسی
MAT	chataa'ee	چٹائی
BAG	thailee	تھَیلی
COT	palang	پلنگ
SIEVE	chhalnee	چھلنی
TUMBLER	gilaas	گِلاس
SPITTOON	ugaldaan	اُگالدان
STRING	rassee	رسّی
NEEDLE	soo'ee	سُوئی
BALANCE	taraazu	ترازُو
CLOCK	gharee	گھڑی

METALS
(Dhatain) دھاتیں

ENGLISH	ROMAN	URDU
IRON	lohaa	لوہا
GOLD	sonaa	سونا
SILVER	chaandee	چاندی
BRASS	peetal	پیتل
LEAD	seesah	سیسہ
STEEL	faulaad	فولاد
COPPER	taambaa	تانبا
MINE	kaan	کان
ZINC	jast	جست
TIN	raangaa	رانگا
BELLMETAL	kaansaa	کانسا
COAL	kooyalaa	کوئلہ
SULPHUR	gandhak	گندھک
WHITE LEAD	qalahee, safaida	قلعی،سفیدا

94

EDIBLES

(Khaane kee cheezen) کھانے کی چیزیں

FOOD	giza	غذا
BREAKFAST	nashtah	ناشتہ
LUNCH	do pahar ka khana	دوپہرکاکھانا
DINNER	raat ka khaanaa	رات کاکھانا
WATER	paanee	پانی
TEA	chaa'e	چائے
RICE	chaawal	چاوَل
GRAIN	daanah	دانہ
CORN	makki, anaaj	مکّی،اَناج
WHEAT	geho'n	گیہوں
BARLEY	jau	جَو
FLOUR	aataa	آٹا
MEAT	gosht	گوشت
FISH	machhlee	مچھلی
BREAD	rotee	روٹی

95

SOUP	*shorbah*	شوربہ
MILK	*doodh*	دُودھ
CURD	*dahee*	دہی
BUTTER	*makkhan*	مکّھن
BUTTER-MILK	*chhaachh*	چھاچھ
CREAM	*malaa'ee*	مَلائی
SUGAR	*cheenee*	چینی
EGG	*anḍaa*	اَنڈا
PICKLE	*achaar*	اچار
JAM	*murabbah*	مُرَبّہ
HONEY	*shahad*	شہد
ICE	*baraf*	بَرف
ONION	*pyaaz*	پیاز
OIL	*tel*	تیل
SWEETMEAT	*mitthaa'ee*	مِٹھائی
BEVERAGE	*sharbat*	شَربَت

PLACE
جگہ (Jagah)

NATION	qaum	قوم
COUNTRY	mulk	مُلک
PROVINCE	soobah	صُوبہ
DISTRICT	zilah	علاقہ، ضلع
CITY	shahr	شہر
TOWN	qasbah	قصبہ
VILLAGE	gaaoun	گاؤں
LANE	gali	گلی
WAY	raastah	راستہ
PLAIN	maidaan	مَیدان
STREET	koochah	کُوچہ
FOREST	jangal	جَنگل
INN	saraaye	سَرائے
GRAVEYARD	qabrastaan	قبرستان

BUILDING

عِمارت (Imarat)

FOUNDATION	bunyaad	بُنیاد
FLOOR	farsh	فرش
HOUSE	makaan	مکان
ROOM	kamrah	کمرہ
KITCHEN	bawarchi khaanah	باورچی خانہ
BATHROOM	ghusal khaanah	غُسل خانہ
URINAL	peshaab khaanah	پیشاب خانہ
DRAWING ROOM	beithak	بَیٹھک
VERANDAH	baraamdah	برآمدہ
COURTYARD	sahan	صحن
COMPOUND	ahaatah	احاطہ
BALCONY	baalaa khaanah	بالا خانہ
BRICK	eent	اینٹ
STONE	patthar	پتّھر

LIME	choonaa	چُونا
SAND	baaloo	بالُو
WALL	deewaar	دیوار
STAIR	seerhee	سِیڑھی
DOOR	darwaazah	دَروازہ
WINDOW	khirkee	کِھڑکی
ROOF	chhat	چھت
GATE	phaatak	پھاٹک
DOOR FRAME	choukhat	چوکھٹ
DOOR SILL	dehleez	دہلیز
CHIMNEY	dhuwaa'n kush	دُھواں کش
DRAIN	moree	موری
HUT	jhonpree	جھونپڑی
NICHE	taaq	طاق
GARDEN	baagh	باغ
LAND	zameen	زمین

AGRICULTURE

(Khetee baaṛee) کھیتی باڑی

CULTIVATOR	kisaan	کسان
LANDHOLDER	zameendaar	زمیندار
LOAN	qarz	قرض
MUD	keechar	کیچڑ
FIELD	khet	کھیت
PLANTER	baghbaan	باغبان
PLOUGH	hal	ہل
TO PLOUGH	hal joutnaa	ہل جوتنا
SEED	beej	بیج
PLANT	pauda	پَودا
CANAL	nahar	نہر
IRRIGATION	aabpasshee	آبپاشی
CROP	fasal	فصل
TO SOW	bona	بونا

FRUIT

(Phal) پھل

MANGO	aam	آم
PLANTAIN	kelaa	کیلا
ORANGE	santarah	سنترہ
FIG	anjeer	انجیر
APPLE	seb	سیب
GUAVA	amrood	اَمرُود
PINEAPPLE	anannaas	اَنّاس
POMEGRANATE	anaar	انار
GRAPE	angoor	انگُور
LEMON	neeboo	نیبُو
PEAR	naashpaatee	ناشپاتی
MELON	kharboozah	خربُوزہ
WATER MELON	tarboozah	تربُوزہ
DATE	khajoor	کھجُور

VEGETABLES

(Subzian) سبزیاں

POTATO	aalu	آلو
CORROT	gaajar	گاجر
CABBAGE	gobhee	گوبھی
CAULIFLOWER	phool gobhee	پھول گوبھی
COCOANUT	naaryel	ناریل
CUCUMBER	kheeraa	کھیرا
PEA	maṭar	مَٹر
ONION	pyaaz	پیاز
TAMARIND	imlee	اِملی
PUMPKIN	kaddoo	کدّو
SPINACH	paalak	پالک
MINT	pudeenaa	پودینہ
BRINJAL	baingan	بینگن
CHILLI	mirch	مِرچ

102

EDUCATION
(T'aleem) تعلیم

TEACHER	*ustaad*	اُستاد
STUDENT	*taalib-e-ilm*	طالِبِ علم
STUDY, KNOWLEDGE	*ilm*	علم
SCHOOL	*madrasah*	مدرسہ
CLASS	*darjah*	درجہ
EXAMINATION	*imtihaan*	اِمتحان
QUESTION	*sawaal*	سَوال
ANSWER	*jawaab*	جواب
EXAMPLE	*missaal*	مِثال
CHOICE	*pasand*	پسند
PRESENCE	*haazree*	حاضری
ABSENCE	*ghair haazree*	غیر حاضری
COMPOSITION	*tasneef*	تصنیف
COMPETITION	*muqaablah*	مُقابلہ

103

EXERCISE	mashq	مشق
LETTER (alphabet)	haraf	حرف
PRONUNCIATION	talaffuz	تلفّظ
SPELLING	hijjaa	ہجّا
SENTENCE	fiqrah	فِقرہ
MEANING	m'ane	معنی
METHOD	tareeqah	طَریقہ
ORAL	zabaanee	زبانی
MAP	naqshah	نقشہ
POEM	nazm	نظم
TEST	aazmaaish	آزمائش
PERCENT	fisadee	فِیصدی
LANGUAGE	zabaan	زبان
PUPIL	shaagird	شاگِرد
LESSON	sabaq	سبق
RESULT	nateejah	نتیجہ

OCCUPATION

(Peshah) پیشہ

SERVANT	naukar	نوکر
MASTER	aaqaa	آقا
THIEF	chor	چور
TRAVELLER	musaafer	مُسافر
SLAVE	ghulaam	غُلام
TEACHER	ustaad	اُستاد
MERCHANT	saudaagar	سَوداگر
JEWELLER	jauharee	جَوہری
SPY	jaasoos	جاسُوس
DOORKEEPER	darbaan	دَربان
DRIVER	gaareebaan	گاڑی بان
BOOKSELLER	kitaabfarosh	کِتاب فروش
WASHERMAN	dhobee	دھوبی
TAILOR	darjee	دَرزی

OILMAN	*teli*	تیلی
BETELSELLER	*tanboli*	تنبولی
GOLDSMITH	*sunaar*	سُنار
CARPENTER	*barha'ee*	بڑھئی
MESSENGER	*qaasid*	قاصِد
MASON	*raaj*	راج
PLAYER	*khilaari*	کھلاڑی
CULTIVATOR	*kisaan*	کِسان
PEON	*chapraasi*	چپراسی
BROKER	*dallaal*	دلّال
BANKER	*sarraaf*	صرّاف
BARBER	*hajjaam*	حجّام
BLACKSMITH	*lohaar*	لُوہار
MINISTER	*wazeer*	وزیر
BOATMAN	*mallaah*	ملّاح
BUTCHER	*qasaa'ee*	قصائی

106

COLOURS
رنگ *(Rang)*

WHITE	safaid	سفید
BLACK	kaala	کالا
BLUE	neela	نیلا
GREEN	hara	ہرا
RED	laal	لال
YELLOW	peela	پیلا
PALE	zard	زرد
PINK	gulaabi	گلابی
ORANGE	naarangi	نارنگی
CRIMSON	qirmizi	قرمزی
GREY	bhoora	بھورا
BROWN	baadami	بادامی
DARK	gahra	گہرا
LIGHT	halka	ہلکا

107

ORDINALS

(Aadaad tarteebi) اعداد ترتیبی

FIRST	pahlaa	پہلا
SECOND	doosraa	دُوسرا
THIRD	teesraa	تیسرا
FOURTH	chauthaa	چَوتھا
FIFTH	paanchwaa'n	پانچواں
SIXTH	chhataa	چھٹا
SEVENTH	saatwaa'n	ساتواں
EIGHTH	aathwaa'n	آٹھواں
NINTH	nawaa'n	نَواں
TENTH	daswaa'n	دَسواں
ELEVENTH	giyaarahwaa'n	گیارہواں

Ordinal numbers, from seven upwards, are regularly formed by adding 'waa'n' واں. It changes according to the number and gender.

For example:

daswaan (m.), daswen (m.pl.), dasween (f. sing. & pl.)

108

NUMERALS

(Aadad) اعداد

Urdu numerals ۱ ۲ ۳ ۴ ۵ ۶ ۷ ۸ ۹ ۱۰

1	2	3	4	5
ēk	*dō*	*teen*	*chaar*	*paañch*
ایک	دو	تین	چار	پانچ
6	7	8	9	10
chhē	*saat*	*aath*	*naọ*	*das*
چھ	سات	آٹھ	نو	دس
11	12	13	14	15
giàrah	*bārah*	*tērah*	*chaudah*	*pandrah*
گیارہ	بارہ	تیرہ	چودہ	پندرہ
16	17	18	19	20
sōlah	*satrah*	*athārah*	*unnis*	*bīs*
سولہ	ستره	اٹھاره	اُنیس	بیس
21	22	23	24	25
ekkis	*bāis*	*tēis*	*chaubis*	*pachis*
اکیس	بائیس	تئیس	چوبیس	پچیس
26	27	28	29	30
chhabbīs	*sattāis*	*atthāis*	*untīs*	*tīs*
چھبیس	ستائیس	اٹھائیس	اُنتیس	تیس

31	32	33	34	35
ektīs	*battīs*	*teñtīs*	*chauntīs*	*paintīs*
اکتیس	بتیس	تینتیس	چونتیس	پینتیس

36	37	38	39	40
chhattīs	*saiñtīs*	*artīs*	*untālīs*	*chālīs*
چھتیس	سینتیس	اڑتیس	انتالیس	چالیس

41	42	43	44	45
ektālīs	*baiālīs*	*teñtālīs*	*chayalīs*	*paiñtālīs*
اکتالیس	بیالیس	تینتالیس	چوالیس	پینتالیس

46	47	48	49	50
chhiālīs	*saintālīs*	*artālīs*	*unchās*	*pachās*
چھیالیس	سینتالیس	اڑتالیس	اونچاس	پچاس

51	52	53	54	55
ekiāwan	*bāwan*	*tirpan*	*chawwan*	*pachpan*
اکیاون	باون	ترپن	چون	پچپن

56	57	58	59	60
chhappan	*sattāwan*	*athāwan*	*unsāth*	*saath*
چھپن	ستاون	اٹھاون	اُنسٹھ	ساٹھ

61	62	63	64	65
eksath	*bāsath*	*tirsath*	*chaunsath*	*paiñsath*
اکسٹھ	باسٹھ	ترسٹھ	چونسٹھ	پینسٹھ

66	67	68	69	70
chhiasath	*sarsath*	*arsath*	*unhattar*	*sattar*
چھیاسٹھ	سرسٹھ	اڑسٹھ	انہتر	ستر

110

71	72	73	74	75
ekhattar	bahattar	tihattar	chohattar	pachhattar
اکہتّر	بہتّر	تہتّر	چوہتّر	پچھتّر

76	77	78	79	80
chhihattar	sathattar	athattar	unnāsi	assī
چھہتّر	ستتّر	اٹھہتّر	اُناسی	اَسّی

81	82	83	84	85
ekiāsī	baiāsī	tirāsī	chorāsī	pachāsī
اکیاسی	بیاسی	تراسی	چوراسی	پچاسی

86	87	88	89	90
chhiāsī	sattāsī	athāsī	navāsī	navē
چھیاسی	ستاسی	اٹھاسی	نواسی	نوے

91	92	93	94	95
ekiānvē	bānvē	tirānvē	chorānvē	pachānvē
اکیانوے	بانوے	ترانوے	چورانوے	پچانوے

96	97	98	99	100
chhiānvē	sattānvē	athānvē	ninānvē	sau
چھیانوے	ستانوے	اٹھانوے	ننانوے	سَو

101	One hundred and one	ek sau ek	ایک سو ایک	۱۰۱
102	One hundred and two	ek sau do	ایک سو دو	۱۰۲
200	Two hundred	do sau	دوسو	۲۰۰
1000	Thousand	hazaar	ہزار	۱۰۰۰
1001	One thousand and one	ek hazaar ek	ایک ہزار ایک	۱۰۰۱

1010	One thousand and ten	*ek hazaar das*	۱۰۱۰ ایک ہزار دس
10,000	Ten thousand	*das hazaar*	۱۰،۰۰۰ دس ہزار
100,000	Hundred thousand	*Lakh*	۱۰۰،۰۰۰ لاکھ
1,000,000	Million	*das lakh*	۱،۰۰۰،۰۰۰ دس لاکھ
10,000,000	Ten Million	*karor*	۱۰،۰۰۰،۰۰۰ کروڑ

FRACTIONS
(Kasarien) کسریں

Quarter	*paaw*	پاؤ
Half	*aadhaa, aadh*	آدھا، آدھ
Three Fourth	*paune, paun*	پَونے، پَون
One and a quarter	*sawaa*	سَوا
One and a half	*derh*	ڈیڑھ
One and three-quarters	*paune do*	پَونے دو
Two and a quarter	*sawaa do*	سَوا دو
Two and a half	*dhaa'ee*	ڈھائی
Two and three-quarters	*paune teen*	پَونے تین
Three and a quarter	*sawaa teen*	سَوا تین
Three and a half	*saarhe teen*	سارھے تین
Three and three-quarters	*paune chaar*	پَونے چار

112

LESSON 10
MODEL SENTENCES

You come.	تم آؤ۔
You don't come.	تم مت آؤ۔
You come tomorrow.	تم کل آنا۔
You don't come tomorrow.	تم کل نہ آنا۔
Please come.	آپ آئیے۔
Please come tomorow.	آپ کل آئیے گا۔
Do (it) in the evening.	(یہ) شام کو کرنا۔
Bring my handkerchief.	میرا رومال لاؤ۔
You sit there.	تم وہاں بیٹھو۔
Please sit on the chair.	آپ کرسی پر بیٹھئے۔
Don't speak here.	یہاں مت بولو۔
Never tell a lie.	کبھی جھوٹ نہ بولنا۔
It is bad to tell lies.	جھوٹ بولنا برا ہے۔
He doesn't know how to read.	اسے پڑھنا نہیں آتا۔

113

I am a teacher.	میں ایک استاد ہوں۔
She is in that class.	وہ اس جماعت میں ہے۔
Who is there?	وہاں کون ہے۔
They are in Lucknow.	وہ لکھنؤ میں ہیں۔
Are you there?	کیا تم وہاں ہو؟
Where were you?	تم کہاں تھے؟
I was in Chennai.	میں چنئی میں تھا۔
Mother was in the kitchen.	ماں باورچی خانے میں تھی۔
My brother was at home.	میرا بھائی گھر پر تھا۔
She was in the Post Office.	وہ ڈاک خانے میں تھی۔
Yesterday you were in the field.	کل تم کھیت میں تھے۔
Tomorrow he will be at Ooty.	کل وہ اوٹی میں ہوگا۔
She will be here.	وہ یہاں ہوگی۔
They will be in the train.	وہ ریل گاڑی میں ہوں گے۔
Where will you be tomorow?	کل تم کدھر ہوں گے؟
The price of his pen is much.	اس کے قلم کا دام زیادہ ہے۔
All these are his.	یہ سب اس کے ہیں۔
Today we will get our ration.	ہماری رسد آج ملے گی۔

114

She is my mother.	یہ میری ماں ہے۔
What is your name?	تمہارا نام کیا ہے؟
My father is not here.	میرے والد یہاں نہیں ہیں۔
It is his village.	یہ اس کا گاؤں ہے۔
India is our homeland.	بھارت ہمارا وطن ہے۔
Bring my book.	میری کتاب لاؤ۔
Is he your friend?	کیا وہ تمہارا دوست ہے؟
Give the rent of my house today.	آج میرے گھر کا کرایہ دے دو۔
You learn Urdu.	تم اردو سیکھتے ہو۔
What do you read?	تم کیا پڑھتے ہو؟
I take bath.	میں غسل کرتا ہوں۔
He reads newspaper.	وہ اخبار پڑھتا ہے۔
She went to the hospital.	وہ اسپتال گئی۔
When did they go to Mumbai.	وہ ممبئی کب گئے؟
I came here last week.	میں پچھلے ہفتے یہاں آیا۔
Did you come from the library?	کیا تم کتب خانے سے آئے؟
When did you return?	تم کب لوٹے؟

He is in the habit of telling lies.	وہ جھوٹ بولا کرتا ہے۔
She was in the habit of coming here.	وہ یہاں آیا کرتی تھی۔
They are in the habit of meeting there.	وہ وہاں ملا کرتے ہیں۔
We are in the habit of going there.	ہم وہاں جایا کرتے ہیں۔
I am in the habit of reading books.	میں کتابیں پڑھا کرتا ہوں۔
Are you in the habit of going alone?	کیا آپ اکیلے جایا کرتے ہیں؟
He was in the habit of coming with me.	وہ میرے ساتھ آیا کرتا تھا۔
You are in the habit of seeing Cinema daily.	تم روز سینما دیکھا کرتے ہو۔
I was in the habit of listening to the radio.	میں ریڈیو سنا کرتا تھا۔
He is in the habit of doing exercise daily.	وہ روز ورزش کیا کرتا ہے۔
Who is in the habit of drinking wine?	کون شراب پیا کرتا ہے؟
She is in the habit of awaiting me daily.	وہ روز میرا انتظار کیا کرتی ہے۔
He is in the habit of shaving daily in the morning.	وہ روز صبح حجامت کیا کرتا ہے۔
I wish to see your mother.	میں آپ کی ماں سے ملنا چاہتا ہوں۔
What do you wish to buy?	تم کیا خریدنا چاہتے ہو؟
Come to my house to get your book.	تم اپنی کتاب لینے میرے گھر آؤ۔

116

A woman has come to cook.	کھانا پکانے کے واسطے ایک عورت آئی ہے
She is not ugly to look.	وہ دیکھنے میں بدصورت نہیں لگتی۔
I shall give you.	میں تم کو دوں گا۔
When will she come?	وہ کب آئے گی؟
He will not do this work.	وہ یہ کام نہیں کرے گا۔
The servant will bring water.	نوکر پانی لائے گا۔
They will return today (f).	وہ آج واپس آئیں گی۔
We shall go to Taj Mahal.	ہم تاج محل چلیں گے۔
Two men were going to Mumbai.	دو آدمی ممبئی جا رہے تھے۔
Women were learning.	عورتیں سیکھ رہی تھیں۔
What was he doing there?	وہ وہاں کیا کر رہا تھا؟
He had come yesterday.	وہ کل آیا تھا۔
I have eaten a mango.	میں نے ایک آم کھایا ہے۔
I had eaten two mangoes.	میں نے دو آم کھائے تھے۔
He has written a letter to him.	اس نے اسے خط لکھا ہے۔
Mohan had gone to Saleem.	موہن سلیم کے پاس گیا تھا۔
Mother has come.	ماں آئی ہے۔
We have seen him there.	ہم نے اسے وہاں دیکھا ہے۔
I have studied Urdu.	میں نے اردو سیکھی ہے۔

He was not there.	وہ وہاں نہیں تھا۔
If you do not come there I too will not go.	اگر تم نہ آتے تو میں بھی نہیں جاتا۔
He does not come every day.	وہ روز روز نہیں آتا۔
We shall not come tomorrow.	ہم کل نہیں آئینگے۔
It is not mine.	یہ میرا نہیں ہے۔
He does not go to his house.	وہ اپنے گھر نہیں جاتا۔
Why didn't he come?	وہ کیوں نہیں آیا؟
He wrote a letter.	اس نے ایک خط لکھا۔
A letter was written by him.	اس نے ایک خط لکھا ہے۔
He was killed by me.	وہ میرے ہاتھ سے مارا گیا۔
It is impossible for me to eat this bread.	مجھ سے یہ روٹی کھائی نہیں جاتی۔
I cannot sleep here.	مجھ سے یہاں سویا نہیں جاتا۔
I am helpless to play now.	اب مجھ سے کھیلا نہیں جاتا۔
Is this the best book?	کیا یہ سب سے اچھی کتاب ہے؟
This room is bigger than that.	یہ کمرہ اس سے بڑا ہے۔
They will do better work than this.	اس سے وہ اچھا کام کرینگے۔
Even the poorest man will not eat this rice.	غریب سے غریب آدمی بھی یہ چاول نہیں کھائیگا۔
It is the lowest price.	یہ کمترین دام ہے۔

118

This is a good dog. یہ اچھا کتا ہے۔

I will buy another one better than this. میں اس سے اچھا دوسرا ایک خریدونگا۔

This boy is better than that. یہ لڑکا اس سے اچھا ہے۔

This is the biggest table in this room. یہ اس کمرے کی سب سے بڑی میز ہے۔

This cot is smaller than that. یہ پلنگ اس سے چھوٹا ہے۔

He came in when I was reading. جب میں پڑھ رہا تھا تب وہ آیا۔

He was not here when I came. جب میں آیا تب وہ یہاں نہیں تھا۔

I was in the office when he came. جب وہ آیا تب میں دفتر میں تھا۔

That man who came here yesterday is my friend. کل جو یہاں آیا وہ میرا دوست ہے۔

Now call the man who wants to go. اب اس آدمی کو بلاؤ جو جانا چاہتا ہے۔

Tell me whatever you know. جو کچھ جانتے ہو مجھے بتاؤ۔

This is the man whose house is in the city. وہ آدمی جس کا گھر شہر میں ہے۔

He went to his house. وہ اپنے گھر گیا۔

I met my brother. میں اپنے بھائی سے ملا۔

Please come. تشریف لائیے۔

Please like it. اسے پسند فرمائیے۔

Please tell, what do you like? فرمائیے، آپ کیا چاہتے ہیں؟

Please sit. تشریف رکھیے۔

119

LESSON 11
CONVERSATIONS
FOOD

غذا (Ghiza)

Get our dinner quickly.   ہمارا کھانا جلدی لاؤ۔
– *Hamārā khānā jaldi lāo.*

Look here, this spoon is not clean.   دیکھو یہ چمچہ صاف نہیں ہے۔
– *Dēkho, yeh chamcha saaf nahin hai.*

This meat is underdone.   یہ گوشت اور پکنا ہے۔
– *Yei gosht aur pakna hai.*

This potato is over-cooked.   یہ آلو بہت گل گیا ہے۔
– *Yeh aalu bahut gal gayā hai.*

What fruits are there in the bazaar?   بازار میں کون کون سے پھل ہیں۔
– *Baazar mēn kaun kaun se phal hain?*

This cup is broken.   یہ پیالی ٹوٹی ہوئی ہے۔
– *Yeh piāli tūti huwee hai.*

No sir, it is not broken.   نہیں صاحب! یہ سالم ہے۔
– *Nahin saheb, yeh salim hai.*

Sharpen this knife quickly.   یہ چھری جلدی تیز کرو۔
– *Yeh chhuri jaldi tēz karo.*

Always bring fresh fish.   ہمیشہ تازہ مچھلی لاؤ۔
– *Hamēsha taazi machhli lāo.*

This bread is stale.   یہ روٹی باسی ہے۔
– *Yeh roti bāsi hai.*

Take away the tea tray. چائے کی کشتی لے جاؤ۔
– Chaae ki kashti lejāo.

Clean your hands. اپنا ہاتھ صاف کرو۔
– Apnē haath sāf karo.

Don't put your finger inside the cup. پیالی میں اپنی انگلی مت ڈالو۔
– Piāli mēn apni ūngli mat dālo.

Throw this soup away. یہ شوربہ پھینک دو۔
– Yeh shorbā phēnkdo.

Look here, it smells. دیکھو! اس میں بو آتی ہے۔
– Dēkho, is mēn bu aati hai.

Bring some boiling water. تھوڑا کھولتا پانی لاؤ۔
– Thorā khaultā pāni lāo.

Put some more ice in it. اس میں تھوڑی برف اور ڈالو۔
– Is mēn thori baraf aur dālo.

I shall dine out tonight. آج شام کو میرا کھانا باہر ہے۔
– Aaj shām ko mera khānā bahar hai.

This meat is bad. یہ گوشت خراب ہے۔
– Yeh gosht kharab hai.

Bring breakfast quickly. ناشتہ جلدی لاؤ۔
– Nāshta jāldi lāo.

This cheese smells. اس پنیر میں بو آتی ہے۔
– Is panir mēn bū aati hai.

Don't butter the toast. توس پر مکھن مت لگاؤ۔

— *Tos par makkhan mat lagāo.*

Bring some pepper and salt. تھوڑا نمک اور گل مرچ لاؤ۔

— *Thoṛā namak aur gol mirch lāo.*

I don't like ghi. مجھ کو گھی پسند نہیں ہے۔

— *Mujhko ghī pasand nahīñ hai.*

This orange is very sour. یہ سنگترہ بہت کھٹا ہے۔

— *Yeh saṅgtara bahut khaṭṭa hai.*

This mango is very sweet. یہ آم بہت میٹھا ہے۔

— *Yeh aam bahut mīthā hai.*

This banana is very delicious. یہ کیلا بہت لذیذ ہے۔

— *Yeh kēlā bahut mazēdār hai.*

The monkeynuts are bitter. مونگ پھلیاں کڑوی ہیں۔

— *Mūñgphaliāñ kaṛwi hain.*

This is very tasteless. یہ بہت بے مزہ ہے۔

— *Yeh bahut beamaza hai.*

Is this biscuit salty or sweet? یہ بسکٹ نمکین ہے یا میٹھا ہے؟

— *Yeh biskuṭ namkīn hai yā mīthā hai.*

What time do you want tea, sir? جناب کو چائے کتنے بجے چاہیئے؟

— *Janāb ko chāē kitnē bajē chāhiē?*

I want tea at quarter to five. مجھ کو چائے پونے پانچ بجے چاہیئے۔

— *Mujh ko chāē paunē paanch bajē chāhiē.*

122

TIME
وقت (Waqt)

What time is it?
کیا وقت ہوا ہے؟
— *Kiā waqt huwa hai?*

It is one o'clock.
ایک بجا ہے۔
— *Ēk bajā hai.*

It is two o'clock.
دو بجے ہیں۔
— *Do bajē haiñ.*

Quarter past one.
سوا بجا ہے۔ (سوا ایک نہیں)۔
— *Sawā baja hai (not sawā ēk).*

Half past one.
ڈیڑھ بجا ہے۔ (ساڑھے ایک نہیں)۔
— *Ḍerh baja hai (not sarhe ēk).*

Half past two.
ڈھائی بجے ہیں۔ (ساڑھے دو نہیں)۔
— *Ḍhai bajē haiñ (not sarhē do).*

Quarter to three.
پونے تین بجے ہیں۔
— *Paunē tīn bajē haiñ.*

Quarter past three.
سوا تین بجے ہیں۔
— *Sawā tīn bajē haiñ.*

Half past three.
ساڑھے تین بجے ہیں۔
— *Sārhē tīn bajē haiñ.*

Quarter to four.
پونے چار بجے ہیں۔
— *Paunē chār bajē haiñ.*

It is ten minutes to four.
چار بجنے میں دس منٹ (کم یا باقی) ہیں۔
— *Chār bajnē mēñ das minat (kam ya bāqī) haiñ.*

دس منٹ کم چار بجے ہیں۔
— *Das minat kam chār bajē haiñ.*

It is ten minutes past four. چار بجکر دس منٹ ہوئے ہیں ۔

– *Chār bajkar das minaṭ hūē haiṅ.*

Are you free (or)

Can you spare time? تم کو فرصت ہے؟

– *Tum ko fursat hai?*

I am very busy. ہم کو بہت کام ہے ۔

– *Ham ko bahut kaam hai.*

I have no time to spare. ہم کو فرصت نہیں ہے ۔

– *Ham ko fursat nahiṅ hai.*

Be here in time. وقت پر آنا ۔

– *Waqt par aanā.*

Don't be late. دیر مت کرنا ۔

– *Der mat karnā.*

How long ago? کتنی دیر ہوئی؟ (وقت)

– (If a matter of time) *Kitnī dēr hūī?*

How long ago? کتنے دن ہوئے؟ (دن)

– (If a matter of days) *Kitnē din (ya roz) huai?*

How long will you stay here? تم یہاں کتنے دن ٹھہرو گے؟

– *Tum yāhaṅ kiṭnē din ṭhairogē?*

How long will you stay at Mumbai?

تم ممبئی میں کتنے دن (یا روز) ٹھہرو گے؟

– *Tum Mumbai mēṅ kiṭnē din (ya roz) ṭhairogē?*

124

This clock is ten minutes slow. یہ گھڑی دس منٹ پیچھے ہے۔

– *Yeh gharee das minat pīchhē hai.*

This watch is ten minutes fast. یہ گھڑی دس منٹ آگے ہے۔

– *Yeh ghari das minat āgē hai.*

You are late. تم دیر سے آئے ہو۔

– *Tum dēr sē aaey ho.*

You are early. تم وقت سے پہلے آئے ہو۔

– *Tum waqt sē pahlē aaye ho.*

You never do any thing in time. تم کام وقت پر نہیں کرتے۔

– *Tum kām waqt par nahīň kartē ho.*

Get it ready by Saturday. اس کو سنیچر تک تیار کر دو۔

– *Is ko Sainichar tak taiyār kardo.*

Have you got the watch with you? تمہارے پاس گھڑی ہے؟

– *Tumhārē pās ghari hai?*

We shall be back in a minute. ہم ابھی واپس آتے ہیں۔

– *Ham abhī wāpas aatē haiň.*

How long will you take to make it? تم اس کو کتنی دیر میں بناؤ گے؟

– *Tum is ko kitnī dēr mēň banāogē?*

What do you mean? تمہارا کیا مطلب ہے؟

– *Tumhārā kiā matlab hai?*

Do you understand? تم سمجھتے ہو؟

– *Tum samajhtē ho?*

We do not understand you. ہم تمہاری بات نہیں سمجھتے ہیں ۔

– *Ham tumhārī bāt nahiñ samajhte haiñ.*

We do not believe you. ہم تمہاری بات نہیں مانتے ۔

– *Ham tumhārī bāt nahiñ mānte.*

We trust you. ہم کو تمہارا اعتبار ہے ۔

– *Ham ko tumhāre etbār hai.*

We are sure. ہم کو یقین ہے ۔

– *Ham ko yaqīn hai.*

We don't know. ہم کو معلوم نہیں ۔

– *Ham ko mālūm nahiñ.*

We are right. ہماری بات ٹھیک ہے ۔

– *Hamārī bāt thīk hai.*

You are wrong. تمہاری بات غلط ہے ۔

– *Tumhārī bāt ghalat hai.*

Don't be afraid. ڈرو مت ۔

– *Daro mat.*

Don't make a fool of us. ہم کو بے وقوف مت بناؤ ۔

– *Ham ko bēwāqūf mat banāo.*

Don't bother us. ہم کو دق مت کرو ۔

– *Ham ko diq mat karo.*

Alright, leave it alone. اچھا! اس کو رہنے دو ۔

– *Ach-chhā, is ko rahnē do.*

126

Never mind.
— *Kuchh parwāh nahīñ.*

کچھ پرواہ نہیں ۔

Go and mind your own business.
— *Jāo, apnā kām karo.*

جاؤ۔اپنا کام کرو۔

Is there any answer to it?
— *Is kā kuchh jawāb hai?*

اس کا کچھ جواب ہے؟

No, there is no answer to it.
— *Nahīñ is ka kucch jawāb nahīñ hai.*

نہیں ۔اس کا کچھ جواب نہیں ہے ۔

Put a rupee stamp on it.
— *Is par ēk rupiya kā tikat lagāo.*

اس پر ایک روپیہ کا ٹکٹ لگاؤ۔

Post this letter.
— *Yeh khat dāk mēñ dālo.*

یہ خط ڈاک میں ڈالو۔

What's up?
— *Kīa hūā?*

کیا ہوا؟

Don't shout.
— *Chillāo mat.*

چلّا وَمت ۔

Shut up. (or) Be quiet.
— *Chup raho.*

چپ رہو۔

Don't chatter.
— *Bak bak mat karo.*

بک بک مت کرو۔

It is useless.
— *Yeh bēfāida hai.*

یہ بے فائدہ ہے ۔

We shall ride (a horse).
— *Ham ghorē par sawari karaiñgē.*

ہم گھوڑے پر سواری کریں گے ۔

127

We shall drive. ہم گاڑی میں جائیں گے ۔

– *Ham gārī men jāēngē.*

We shall go by car. ہم موٹر میں جائیں گے ۔

– *Ham motar men jāēngē.*

We shall go on foot. ہم پیدل جائیں گے ۔

– *Ham paidal jāēngē.*

There is one rupee short. ایک روپیہ کم ہے ۔

– *Ēk rupiya kam hai.*

I like you for it. مجھ کو تمھاری یہ بات پسند ہے ۔

– *Mujh ko tumhārī yeh bāt pasand hai.*

Get that man out of my sight. اس آدمی کو میرے سامنے سے ہٹا دو ۔

– *Us ādmī ko mērē sāmnē sē haṭā do.*

Why don't you speak, when you are spoken to?

جب کوئی بولے تو جواب کیوں نہیں دیتے ہو؟

– *Jab koī bolē to jawāb kion nahin dētē ho?*

It comes to the same thing. یہ ایک ہی بات ہے ۔

– *Yeh ēk hī bāt hai.*

I cannot get my tongue round this word.

یہ لفظ میری زبان پر نہیں چڑھتا ۔

– *Yeh lafz mērī zabān par nahin charhtā.*

But me no buts. ہم سے اگر مگر مت کرو ۔

– *Ham sē agar magar mat karo.*

128

MY HOUSE
(Meraa ghar) میرا گھر

It is my house. — یہ میرا گھر ہے۔
Yeh meraa ghar hai.

It is beautiful. — یہ خوبصورت ہے۔
Yeh khoobsoorat hai.

It is a new house. — یہ نیا گھر ہے۔
Yeh nayaa ghar hai

It is not small. — یہ چھوٹا نہیں ہے۔
Yeh chhoṭaa nahenn hai.

There are five rooms in it. — اس میں پانچ کمرے ہیں۔
Is me'n paanch kamre hain.

It is bathroom. — یہ غسل خانہ ہے۔
Yeh ghusalkhaanah hai.

That is urinal. — وہ پیشاب خانہ ہے۔
Woh peshaabkhaanah hai.

There is no veranda in it. — اس میں برآمدہ نہیں ہے۔
Is me'n barramdah naheen hai.

It is my room. — یہ میرا کمرہ ہے۔
Yeh meraa kamrah hai.

Here I study. — یہاں میں پڑھتا ہوں۔
Yahan main parhta hoon.

My watch is not correct. — میری گھڑی ٹھیک نہیں ہے۔
Meri gharee ṭheek nahee'n hai.

129

What is the time now?	اب کتنے بجے ہیں؟
— Ab kitne baje hai'n?	
It is being eight O'clock..	اب آٹھ بج رہے ہیں۔
— Ab aath baj rahe hain.	
It is ten to two.	دو بجنے میں دس منٹ ہیں۔
— Do bajne men das minit hai'n.	
It is ten past two.	دو بج کر دس منٹ ہوئے ہیں۔
— Do baj kar das minit huye hai'n.	
It is quarter past one.	سوا بجا ہے۔
— Sawaa bajaa hai.	
It is quarter past two.	سوا دو بجے ہیں۔
— Sawaa do baje hai'n.	
It is quarter past three.	سوا تین بجے ہیں۔
— Sawaa teen baje hai'n.	
It is half past one.	ڈیڑھ بجا ہے۔
— Derh baja hai.	
It is half past two.	ڈھائی بجے ہے۔
— Dhaa'i baje hai'n.	
It is quarter to two.	پونے دو بجے ہیں۔
— Paune do baje hai'n.	
At what time?	کتنے بجے؟
— Kitne baje?	
At One O'clock.	ایک بجے۔
— Ek baje.	

IN THE MARKET
(baazaar main) بازار میں

Where is the shopkeeper?   دوکاندار کہاں ہے؟
— *Dookaandaar kahaa'n hai?*

(He) is coming.   آرہا ہے۔
— *Aa rahaa hai.*

Please come; what do you want?   آئیے صاحب،
— *Aa'iye ṣaahab, kyaa chaahiye?*   کیا چاہئے؟

(I) want mango.   آم چاہئے۔
— *Aam chaahiye.*

How many?   کتنے؟
— *Kitnae?*

These mangoes are not good.   یہ آم اچھے نہیں ہیں۔
— *Yeh aam achchhe nahee'n hai'n.*

I want fresh mango.   مجھے تازہ آم چاہئے۔
— *Mujhe taazah aam chaahiye.*

Sir, these mangoes?   یہ آم، صاحب؟
— *Yeh aam ṣaahab?*

These are very small.   یہ بہت چھوٹے ہیں۔
— *Yeh bahoot chhoṭe hai'n.*

But very sweet, sir.   لیکن بہت میٹھے ہیں، صاحب۔
— *Lekin bahoot meeteh hai'n ṣaahab.*

131

What is the price?

دام کیا ہے۔

– *Daam kyaa hai.*

Thirty rupees per kilo.

تیس روپئے کلو۔

– *Tees rupye kilo.*

It is very dear.

بہت مہنگا ہے۔

– *Bahut mah'nga hai.*

But it is of very good quality.

لیکن بڑھیا قسم کا ہے۔

– *Lekin bariyaa kism kaa hai.*

(It) came only this morning.

آج صبح ہی آیا ہے۔

– *Aaj subah hee aayaa hai.*

Give two kilos.

دو کلو دو۔

– *Do kilo do.*

How much these grapes are?

یہ انگور کیسے؟ (دو گے)

– *Yeh angoor kaise? (dogai)*

Twenty rupees per kilo.

بیس روپئے کلو۔

– *Bees rupye kilo.*

Give half kilo.

آدھا کلو دو۔

– *Aadhaa kilo do.*

Shall I give water-melon?

یہ تربوز دوں؟

– *Tarbooz doo'n?*

No, take these rupees.

نہیں، یہ روپئے لو۔

– *Nahee'n, yah rupye lo.*

POST-OFFICE
(Ḍaak khaanah) ڈاک خانہ

Where is the post-office?

– Ḍaak khaanah kidhar hai?

ڈاک خانہ کدھر ہے؟

How far is it?

– Kitnee door hai?

کتنی دور ہے؟

Give me four envelopes.

– Chaar lifaafe do.

چار لفافے دو۔

Give me ten stamps of ten rupees.

– Das rupye ke das ṭikaṭ do.

دس روپے کے دس ٹکٹ دو۔

Take this letter to the post-office.

– Yeh khat daak khaanah le jaa'o.

یہ خط ڈاک خانہ لے جاؤ۔

What is his address?

– U's kaa pataa kyaa hai?

اس کا پتہ کیا ہے؟

Write his address on the envelope.

– Lifaafe par us kaa patah likho.

لفافہ پر اس کا پتہ لکھو۔

Give this telegram to him.

– U's ko yah taar de do.

اس کو یہ تار دے دو۔

Bring the receipt.

– Raseed laa'o.

رسید لاؤ۔

This letter is not mine.

– Yeh khat mera nahee'n hai.

یہ خط میرا نہیں ہے۔

133

RAILWAY STATION

ریل گاہ (Railgaah)

The train has left. گاڑی چھوٹ گئی۔
— *Gaaree choot gayee.*

At what time the Delhi-mail arrives? دلّی میل کتنے
— *Dillee-mail kitne baji pahunchegee?* بجے پہنچے گی؟

When will the train depart? گاڑی کب روانہ ہوگی؟
— *Gaaree kab rawaanah hogee?*

The train is coming late. گاڑی دیر سے آرہی ہے۔
— *Gaari der se aa rahee hai.*

Porter! come here. قلی ادھر آؤ۔
— *Qulee idhar aa'o.*

Take this box. یہ پیٹی لو۔
— *Yeh petee lo.*

The bedding is over there. ادھر اوپر بستر ہے۔
— *Udhar oopar bistar hai.*

I want a taxi. مجھے ایک ٹیکسی چاہئے۔
— *Mujhe ek teksee chaahiye.*

How much is the fare? کرایہ کتنا ہے؟
— *Kiraayah kitna hai.*

Well take ten rupees more. اچھا دس روپئے زیادہ لو۔
— *Achchaa, Das rupiye ziyaadah lo.*

Now drive to Chandni Chowk. اب چاندنی چوک
— *Ab Chaandini Chowk le chalo.* لے چلو۔

134

HOTEL
هوٹل (Hoṭal)

Is there any good hotel?   یہاں کوئی اچھا ہوٹل ہے؟
– *Yahha'n ko'ee achchaa hotel hai?*

I want a room.   مجھے ایک کمرہ چاہیئے۔
– *Mujhe ek kamrah chaahiye.*

Only for three days.   صرف تین دن کے لئے۔
– *Sirf teen din ke liye.*

Is there bath-room?   کیا غسل خانہ بھی ہے؟
– *Kyaa ghusalkhaanah bhee hai?*

How much is the rent?   کرایہ کتنا ہے؟
– *Kiraayah kitnaa hai?*

Is hot water available?   کیا گرم پانی ملے گا؟
– *Kyaa garam paanee milegaa.*

Where is my room?   میرا کمرہ کدھر ہے؟
– *Meraa kamrah kidhar hai.*

What is the number of the room?   کمرے کا نمبر کیا ہے؟
– *Kamre ka nambar kyaa hai.*

Where is the bathroom?   غسل خانہ کہاں ہے؟
– *Ghusalkhaanah kahaa'n hai.*

Bring a cup of tea.   ایک پیالی چائے لاؤ۔
– *Ek pyaali chaa'e laa'o.*

135

MEETING
(Mulaqat) ملاقات

Ram: Good morning.   رام: آداب عرض۔

Ram: *Aadab Aradh.*

Ahmad: Good morning. How do you do?

احمد: آداب۔ مزاج شریف۔

Ahmad: *Aadab, Mizaj Shareef?*

Ram: Thank you. I am well.   رام: شکریہ۔ میں اچھا ہوں۔

Ram: *Shukriya. Main achha houn.*

Ahmad: Please sit down. When did you come from Allahabad?

احمد: تشریف رکھیئے۔ آپ الہ آباد سے کب آئے؟

Ahmad: *Tashreef rakhiyeh. Aap Illahbad se kab Aaie?*

Ram: I came here last Monday.

رام: میں گذشتہ پیر کو یہاں آیا۔

Ram: *Main guzishta peer ko yehan aaya.*

Ahmad: I did not know that you were here, otherwise I would have come to see you.

احمد: مجھے نہیں معلوم تھا کہ آپ یہاں تشریف رکھتے ہیں ورنہ میں ملاقات کے لئے ضرور حاضر ہوتا۔

Ahmad: *Mujhe nahi maloom tha ke aap yehan tashreef rakhte hein, warna main mulaqaat ke liye zaroor hazir hota.*

Ram: Would you please come to my place tomorrow?

رام: کیا آپ کل میرے یہاں تشریف لائیں گے؟

Ram: Kiya aap kal mere yahan tashreef laienge?

Ahmad: Thank you for your kindness. I will positively come tomorrow evening.

احمد: آپ کی مہربانی کا شکریہ۔ میں کل شام کو ضرور حاضر ہونگا۔

Ahmad: Aap ki meherbani ka shukriya. Main kal shaam ko zaroor hazir hoenga.

Ram: Is it your own house?

رام: کیا یہ آپ کا ذاتی مکان ہے؟

Ram: Kiya yeh aap ka zati makan hai?

Ahmad: Yes.   احمد: جی ہاں۔

Ahmad: Ji Haan.

Ram: How many rooms are there in this house?

رام: اس مکان میں کتنے کمرے ہیں؟

Ram: Is makan main kitne kamre hain?

Ahmad: There are four rooms and two verandas on ground floor and two rooms on first floor. In addition, there is kitchen and a bathroom. There is a small garden at the back of the house.

احمد: چار کمرے اور دو برآمدے نچلی منزل میں ہیں اور دو کمرے اوپری منزل میں ہیں۔ ان کے علاوہ باورچی خانہ اور غسل خانہ ہے۔ مکان کی پشت پر ایک چھوٹا سا باغ ہے۔

Ahmad: *Chaar kamre aur do baramadeh nichli manzil main hain aur do kamre uperi manzil main hain. In ke alawah bawerchikhana aur ghusal khana hai. Makan ki pusht par ek chhota sa baagh hai.*

Ram: Now I beg leave of you. I have been very pleased to see you.

رام: اب اجازت چاہتا ہوں۔ آپ سے مل کر بڑی خوشی ہوئی۔

Ram: *Ab ijazat chhata houn. Aap se milker badi khushi hoie.*

Ahmad: It is kind of you to visit me. Please have a cup of tea.

احمد: یہ آپ کی عنایت ہے کہ ملاقات کے لئے تشریف لائے۔
ایک پیالی چائے تو پی لیجئے۔

Ahmad: *Yeh aap ki inayet hai ke mulaqaat ke liye tashreef laaie. Ek piyali chai to pi lijiah.*

Ram: Thank you. I have to go to the picture with a friend of mine. I may be late.

رام: شکریہ۔ مجھے ایک دوست کے ساتھ سنیما جانا ہے۔ دیر ہو جائے گی۔

Ram: *Shukriya. Mujhe ek dost ke saath cinema jana hai. der ho jaigee.*

DOCTOR AND PATIENT

(Daktar Aur Mareez) ڈاکٹر اور مریض

Patient: Doctor, I have a severe cold since yesterday, a slight temperature and also a headache.

مریض: ڈاکٹر صاحب مجھے کل سے سخت زکام ہے۔ مجھے کچھ حرارت ہے اور سر میں درد بھی ہے۔

Mareez: Daktar saheb mujhe kal se sakht zukaam hai. Mujhe kuchh hararet hai aur ser main dard bhi hai.

Doctor: I am writing the prescription. Take the medicines regularly. Your cold will disappear in two days. Don't worry.

ڈاکٹر: میں نسخہ لکھ دیتا ہوں۔ دوا باقاعدہ استعمال کیجئے آپ کا زکام دو دن میں ٹھیک ہو جائے گا۔ فکر نہ کریں۔

Daktar: Main nuskhah likh deta hoen. Dawa baqaedah istemal kijiah. Aap ka zukaam do din main theek ho jaiaga. Fikar na karain.

Patient: I did not sleep last night. I had a stomach ache and constipation too.

مریض: میں رات بھر نہں سویا۔ میرے پیٹ میں درد ہے۔ مجھے قبض
بھی ہے۔

Mareez: Main raat bhar nahi soya. Maire pate main dard
hai. Mujhe qabz bhi hai.

Doctor: Suck this tablet slowly. It is good for the ache.
This medicine is good for constipation.

ڈاکٹر: اس ٹکیہ کو آہستہ آہستہ چوسیں۔ یہ درد کے لئے مفید ہے۔ یہ دوا
قبض کے لئے مفید ہے۔

Daktar: Is tikya ko aahaista aahaista choosain. Yeh
dard ke liye mufeed hai. Yeh dawa qabz ke liye
mufeed hai.

Patient: My tooth is also aching.

مریض: میرے دانت میں بھی درد ہے۔

Mareez: Mere dant main bhi dard hai.

Doctor: You should have your tooth extracted. It is no
use filling it.

ڈاکٹر: آپ کو دانت نکلوادینا چاہئیے ۔ پُر کرنے سے کوئی فائدہ نہیں۔

Daktar: Aap ko dant nikalwadaina chahiye. Pur karne
se koie faidah nahi.

140

CINEMA

(Pikcher Haous) پکچر ہاؤس

I like to go to cinema. Cinema and theatre are good pastimes.

میں سینما دیکھنا پسند کرتا ہوں ۔ سینما اور تھیٹر وقت گذارنے کے لئے اچھے ہیں ۔

Main sainama daikhna pasend karta hoen. Sainama aur theatre waqt guzarne ke liye achhe hain.

Students can be benifited by educational films.

تعلیمی فلموں سے طالب علم فائدہ اٹھا سکتے ہیں ۔

Taelimee filmoun se talib-e-ilm faidah utha sakte hain.

Most of the films are entertaining.

زیادہ تر فلمیں تفریحی ہوتی ہیں ۔

Ziyadatar filmain tafrihee hoti hain.

Yesterday I saw a war-film which was very exciting.

کل میں نے ایک جنگی فلم دیکھی جو بڑی سنسنی خیز تھی ۔

Kal main ne ek jangi film daikhi jo badi sansanikhaiz thi.

Indian film industry has made a good progress.

ہندوستان کی فلمی صنعت نے بڑی ترقی کی ہے ۔

Hindustan ki filmi sanait ne badi tareqqi ki hai.

I like entertaining films.

میں تفریحی فلمیں پسند کرتا ہوں ۔

Main tafreehi filmain pasand karta hoen.

141

IN THE SHOPPING CENTRE

(Hama jins dukan main) ہمہ جنس دُکان میں

Customer:	How much per dozen are these bananas?

خریدار: یہ کیلے کتنے میں درجن ہیں؟

Kharidar:	*Yeh kaile kitne main darjan hain?*
Shopkeeper:	They cost twenty rupees per dozen.

دکاندار: یہ بیس روپے درجن ہیں۔

Dukandar:	*Yeh bees rupia darjan hain.*
Customer:	It is expensive. What will you charge after all?

خریدار: یہ تو مہنگے ہیں۔ آخر کیا لوگے؟

Kharidar:	*Yeh to mahenge hain. Aakher kiya loge?*
Shopkeeper:	I will charge four rupees less for you.

دکاندار: میں آپ سے چار روپئے کم لوں گا۔

Dukandar:	*Main aap se chaar rupia kam loenga.*
Customer:	How much per kilo these apples cost?

خریدار: یہ سیب کیسے کیلو ہیں؟

Kharidar:	*Yeh saib kaise kilo hain?*

Shopkeeper: These cost fifteen rupees a kilo.

دکاندار: یہ پندرہ روپیہ کلو ہیں۔

Dukandar: *Yeh pandra rupia kilo hain.*

Customer: These apples are rotten, even if you give them free they are not worth having.

خریدار: یہ سیب خراب ہو چکے ہیں۔ یہ تو مفت بھی مہنگے ہیں۔

Kharidar: *Yeh saib kharab ho chuke hain. Yeh to muft bhi mahenge hain.*

Customer: Where is this cloth from?

خریدار: یہ کپڑا کہاں کا بنا ہے؟

Kharidar: *Yeh kapda kahan ka bana hai?*

Shopkeeper: It has recently been imported from Japan.

دکاندار: یہ ابھی جاپان سے منگایا ہے۔

Dukandar: *Yeh abhi Japan se mangayah hai.*

Customer: But the quality of this cloth is not good. It gets creases soon.

خریدار: لیکن اس کپڑے کی کوالٹی اچھی نہیں ہے۔ شکن جلدی پڑ جاتے ہیں۔

Kharidar: *Laikin is kapde ki kuwalaiti achhi nahi hai. Shiken jaledi pad jate hain.*

143

Customer: How much is this cloth per metre?

خریدار: اس کپڑے کی فی میٹر قیمت کیا ہے؟

Kharidar: Is kapde ki fi mitar qimat kiya hai?

Shopkeeper: It is hundred rupees a metre.

دکاندار: یہ سو روپیہ میٹر ہے۔

Dukandar: Yeh sau rupia mitar hai.

Customer: Well, give me five metres.

خریدار: اچھا پانچ میٹر دے دو۔

Kharidara: Achha, panch mitar de do.

LESSON 12
LETTER WRITING

LETTER - 1

INFORMAL LETTER

Kailash Bhavan,
Mumbai-13,
Date: 8 January, 2004.

My dear Gopal,

Kindly send me back my book, which I had given to you last week, because I want it for my studies.

Yours beloved,
Basheer

خط ۱

غیر رسمی خط

کیلاش بھَون، ممبئی ۔۱۳

تاریخ: ۸؍جنوری ۲۰۰۴ء

میرے پیارے گوپال!

گذشتہ ہفتہ میں نے تم کو جو کتاب دی تھی اسے لوٹا دو گے تو بڑی مہربانی ہوگی۔ مجھے پڑھنے کے لئے چاہئے۔

تمہارا عزیز دوست
بشیر

LETTER - 2

ASKING FOR LOAN

209, Ratanjyoti Bldg.,
Rajindra Place,
New Delhi-8

Dear Ahmed,

My parents came here today in the morning, so I want two hundred rupees. Please send it with this man. Today I shall not come to your house, tomorrow certainly I will come.

Yours friend,
Ramesh

خط ۲

قرض کے لئے گزارش

۲۰۹، رتن جیوتی بلڈنگ،
راجندر پلیس،
نئی دہلی-نمبر ۸

پیارے احمد،

آج صبح میرے والدین یہاں آئے۔ اس لئے مجھے دوسو روپیے چاہئیے۔ مہربانی کرکے اس آدمی کے ہاتھ بھیج دو۔ میں آج تمہارے یہاں نہیں آسکوں گا۔ کل ضرور آؤنگا۔

تمہارا دوست
رمیش

146

LETTER TO FRIEND

8, West Main Road,
Chennai-12.

Dear Friend,

Tomorrow is my birthday, therefore there will be a party in our house at five o'clock in the evening. You must come. Don't forget!

Yours beloved,
Kailash

خط ـ۳

دوست کے نام خط

۸ ـ ویسٹ مین روڈ،
چنئی ـ۱۲

پیارے دوست،

کل میری سالگرہ ہے، اس لئے کل شام پانچ بجے میرے گھر پارٹی ہے۔ تم ضرور آنا ـ بھولنا نہیں!

تمہارا پیارا دوست
کیلاش

LETTER-4

LETTER TO EDITOR

To

The Editor,
Magazine 'Sayaanee'
Sewapura, Bhopal-5.

Dear Sir,

I am sending my annual subscription, Rupees three hundred, by M.O. for 'Sayaanee'. The receipt's number is 301. Please send one magazine from this month onwards.

Yours sincerely,
Mohandas

خط ۴

ایڈیٹر کے نام خط

بخدمت جناب ایڈیٹر صاحب

رسالہ 'سیانی'

سیواپورہ، بھوپال ۵۔

مکرمی،

آپ کے رسالہ 'سیانی' کا سالانہ چندہ تین سو روپے منی آرڈر سے بھیج رہا ہوں۔ رسید کا نمبر ۳۰۱ ہے۔ مہربانی کرکے رسالہ اس مہینے سے ہی بھیجئے۔

آپ کا مخلص

موہن داس

LETTER-5
LETTER TO PUBLISHER

The Manager,
Kitab Mahal,
Patna-4.
Dear Sir,
Kindly send me the following books by V.P.P.

1. Armughaan-e-Urdu
2. Kahanian
3. Burhi Kaaki

Yours faithfully,
Anwaar Ahmad Khan

خط ۵
پبلشر کے نام خط

ناشر

جناب مینجر صاحب،
کتاب محل، پٹنہ ۴
مکرمی،
عرض ہے کہ نیچے لکھی ہوئی کتابیں میرے پتے پر وی۔ پی۔ پی۔ سے
بھیج دیجئے۔
۱۔ ارمغانِ اردو۔
۲۔ کہانیاں۔
۳۔ بوڑھی کاکی۔

آپ کا نیاز مند
انوار احمد خاں

149

LETTER-6

THANKSGIVING LETTER

Dear friend,

Please accept my sincerest gratitude for getting for me a job in the Bengal Chemicals Ltd. You have proved yourself to be a true friend of mine for fixing me up in a decent firm. You have done your duty wonderfully well. It is for me to rise by hard labour and loyalty.

Yours beloved,
John Edwin

خط ۔۶

نامہ برتشکّر

پیارے دوست،

تم نے مجھے بنگال کیمیکل لمیٹڈ میں نوکری دلوا کر جو مہربانی کی ہے۔ اس کے لئے تہہ دِل سے میرا شکریہ قبول کریں۔ ایک عمدہ کمپنی میں مجھے مقرر کروا کر تم نے یہ ثابت کر دیا ہے کہ تم میرے سچّے دوست ہو۔ تم نے اپنا فرض بہت خوبی سے ادا کیا ہے۔ اب تو محنت اور وفاداری سے ترقی کرنا میرا کام ہے۔

تمہارا پیارا دوست

جان ایڈ وِن

LETTER-7
APPLICATION FOR LEAVE

From

      Abbas Ali Khan,
      Typist,
      The Forest Department, Ranchi.

To

      The Director,
      The Forest Department, Ranchi.

Dear Sir,

      As I have to go to Chennai for my eye-operation prescribed, I request you to grant me medical leave for fifteen days from May 2 to May 16. I shall produce a medical certificate at the time of rejoining the duty.

Thanking you,

                      Yours Obediently,
                      Abbas Ali Khan

درخواستِ رخصت

از: عباس علی خاں، ٹائپسٹ
       محکمۂ جنگلات، رانچی۔

الی: بخدمت جناب ڈائریکٹر صاحب،
       محکمۂ جنگلات، رانچی۔

جنابِ عالی،

چونکہ مجھے اپنی آنکھ کے آپریشن کے لئے چنئی جانا ہے۔ لہٰذا درخواست
ہے کہ احقر کو ۲ رمئی تا ۱۶ رمئی، پندرہ دنوں کی رخصت، طبّی بنیاد پر،
عنایت کی جائے۔

دوبارہ کام پر آنے کے وقت اس سلسلہ میں مطلوبہ میڈیکل سرٹیفیکیٹ
پیشِ خدمت کروں گا۔ بصد شکریہ

آپ کا تابعدار
عباس علی خاں

LETTER-8

SON'S LETTER TO FATHER

Mohammed Ahmad,
15, Mahatma Gandhi Road,
Kolkata-700012.

Respected Father,

I hope you are well. I reached here safely on Tuesday. Respected brother was present at the station to receive me. Please don't worry about me. Everything is all right here. Please convey my salam to my mother and best wishes to the sister.

Expecting your blessings.

Your servant
Mohammed Ahmad

لڑکے کا خط باپ کے نام

از: محمد احمد
۱۵، مہاتما گاندھی روڈ،
کولکتہ ۔ ۷۰۰۰۱۲

محترم عالی جناب والد صاحب،

امید ہے مزاج عالی بخیر ہوگا ۔ میں یہاں منگل کو بخیریت تمام
پہونچ گیا ۔ بھائی صاحب مجھے لینے کے لئے اسٹیشن پر موجود تھے ۔
آپ میرے بارے میں کوئی فکر نہ کریں ۔ یہاں اور سب خیریت
ہے ۔ والدہ صاحبہ کی خدمت میں سلام عرض ہے اور بہن کو نیک
خواہشات ۔

دعاؤں کا طالب
آپ کا خادم
محمد احمد

LESSON 13
SHORT STORIES

A LAMP OF A BLIND

There was a blind man. He was daily going to the river in the night and bringing water in an earthen pot. At the time of going and coming he used to have a lamp in his hand. He was blind, so what was the advantage of lamp for him? Having seen that the people were amazed.

One day a man asked him, "O! For you, what is darkness? what is brightness? There is no difference. But why do you have the lamp with you in the night-hour?"

Hearing this the blind man began to smile and said, "This lamp is not for me, but for one who is blind, even though he has good sight; that is, he might not be dashed on me and my earthen pot might not be broken.

Hearing this the man asking, felt ashamed.

مختصر کہانیاں

اندھے کا چراغ

ایک تھا اندھا۔ وہ ایک روز رات ہونے پر پانی بھرنے ندی پر جاتا اور گھڑے میں پانی لاتا تھا۔ وہ آتے جاتے وقت اپنے ہاتھ میں ایک لالٹین رکھتا تھا۔ وہ تو تھا اندھا، لالٹین سے اسے کیا فائدہ؟ یہ دیکھ کر لوگوں کو بڑا تعجب ہوتا تھا۔

ایک دن ایک آدمی نے پوچھا۔ ارے! تیرے لئے کیا اندھیرا کیا اُجالا! دونوں میں کوئی فرق نہیں ہے۔ لیکن تو تو رات میں یہ لالٹین کیوں لئے پھرتا ہے؟

اندھا اس کی یہ بات سن کر مسکرا اٹھا اور کہا۔ ''یہ لالٹین اپنے لئے نہیں، لیکن اس کے لئے ہے جو آنکھیں ہوتے ہوئے بھی اندھا ہوتا ہے، یعنی کہیں مجھ اندھے سے ٹکرا نہ جائے اور میرا گھڑا نہ توڑ دے''۔

یہ سن کر وہ آدمی شرما گیا۔

IDLE SERVANT

Once there was a shopkeeper. His shop was very big. Many servants were working in that shop. One of them was very idle. Daily he used to come late. The shopkeeper was observing the same.

One day the shopkeeper asked the servant, "Why do you come late daily?"

The servant said, "Sir, my watch is not showing the correct time. Please excuse me today. From tomorrow onwards I shall come in time.

After that, one day the servant came late again .The shopkeeper asked him, "Why have you come late again?"

The servant said, "Sir, my watch is not in good condition."

The shopkeeper said, "Well! Get a new watch tomorrow, otherwise I will appoint a new servant."

آلسی نوکر

ایک دوکاندار تھا۔ اس کی دوکان بہت بڑی تھی۔ اس دوکان میں کئی نوکر کام کرتے تھے ان نوکروں میں ایک تھا بڑا آلسی۔ وہ روز دیر سے آتا تھا۔ دوکاندار یہ دیکھتا تھا۔

ایک دن اس نوکر سے دوکاندار نے پوچھا۔"تم روز کیوں دیر سے آتے ہو؟"

نوکر نے بتایا-"صاحب میری گھڑی ٹھیک وقت نہیں بتاتی۔ آج معاف کیجئے۔ کل سے ٹھیک وقت پر آ جاؤں گا۔"

اس کے بعد ایک دن وہ نوکر پھر دیر سے آیا۔ دوکاندار نے اس سے پوچھا-"تم آج پھر دیر سے کیوں آئے ؟"

نوکر نے کہا-"صاحب میری گھڑی ٹھیک نہیں ہے۔"

اس پر دوکاندار نے کہا، کل تم ایک نئی گھڑی خرید لو۔ نہیں تو میں ایک نیا نوکر رکھ لوں گا۔

THE RESULT OF DISPUTE

There was a rat. There was a frog too. Both were friends. One day they had a piece of bread. Having this the two began to dispute.

The rat was desiring, "May I eat the full piece, so the frog couldn't have any bit.

The frog too was desiring, "May I lick the full piece, so the rat could stay in hungry.

There was a she-goat grazing near them. It advised them, "Why are you fighting? Take half-half."

They two did not accept the advice of the she-goat. They were disputing with each other.

A kite was flying above. The sight of it was fallen on them. It was too hungry. So it came down and caught the disputing frog and rat in the claws and took away.

The piece of bread was lying there on the ground.

جھگڑے کا نتیجہ

ایک چوہا تھا۔ ایک مینڈک بھی تھا۔ دونوں دوست تھے۔ ایک دن ان کو روٹی کا ایک ٹکڑا ملا۔ اسے لے کر دونوں جھگڑنے لگے۔

چوہا چاہتا تھا۔ میں پورا ٹکڑا کھا جاؤں، اور مینڈک کو کچھ بھی نہ ملے۔

مینڈک بھی چاہتا تھا کہ میں پورا ٹکڑا چٹ کر جاؤں اور چوہا بھوکا ہی رہ جائے۔

ادھر ایک بکری چر رہی تھی۔ اس نے ان دونوں کو سمجھایا۔ کیوں جھگڑتے ہو؟ آدھا آدھا لے لو۔

دونوں نے بھی اس بکری کی بات نہ مانی۔ آپس میں جھگڑتے ہی رہے۔

اوپر ایک چیل اڑ رہی تھی۔ اس کی نظر ان دونوں پر پڑی وہ بڑی وہ بھوکی تھی۔ اس لئے وہ نیچے آئی اور جھگڑنے والے مینڈک اور چوہے کو اپنے دونوں پنجوں میں دبا کر اڑا لے گئی۔ روٹی کا وہ ٹکڑا وہیں زمین پر پڑا رہ گیا۔

BIRBAL

One day, King Akbar and queen were eating mangoes sitting in the terrace. Eating the mangoes, the King was putting all the stones and the peels by the side of the queen. In the meanwhile Birbal came there.

Just seeing Birbal the King thought of making fun of the queen.

"Have you seen Birbal?" The King said, "What a gourmand this lady is! She has eaten so many mangoes. It is true that she has piled these much stones and peels."

"Oh King ! It is the effect of company."

"What? Has she become gourmand because of my company?" Akbar asked.

"Oh Your Imperial Majesty! Wife always imitates her husband."

Akbar asked, "But, am I gourmand? Peels and stones are on her side. Not any one of them on my side."

Birbal answered, "I am also saying the same thing. Oh King, the queen has eaten only mangoes, but you have not left even the peels and stones."

بیربل

ایک دن اکبر بادشاہ اور بیگم چبوترہ پر بیٹھے آم کھا رہے تھے۔ بادشاہ آم کھا کھا کر چھلکے اور گٹھلیاں بیگم کی طرف رکھتے گئے۔ اتنے میں بیربل وہاں آیا۔

بیربل کو دیکھتے ہی بادشاہ کو خیال آیا کہ اب بیگم کا مذاق اڑاؤں۔

"دیکھا، بیربل!" بادشاہ نے کہا۔ "یہ بیگم کیسی پیٹو ہے! اس نے اتنے سارے آم کھائے ہیں! یہ تو سچ ہے کہ انہوں نے اتنے چھلکوں اور گٹھلیوں کا ڈھیر لگا دیا ہے۔"

"بادشاہ! یہ تو صحبت کا اثر ہے۔" بیربل نے کہا۔ "کیا؟ میری صحبت کی وجہ سے یہ پیٹو بن گئی ہے؟" اکبر بادشاہ نے پوچھا۔

"جہاں پناہ! ہمیشہ بیوی اپنے شوہر کی ہی نقل کرتی ہے۔" اکبر نے کہا "لیکن کیا میں پیٹو ہوں؟ چھلکے اور گٹھلیاں تو اس کی طرف ہیں۔ میری طرف تو ایک بھی نہیں ہے۔"

بیربل نے جواب دیا، "میں بھی تو یہی کہہ رہا ہوں، بادشاہ! بیگم صاحبہ نے تو صرف آم کھائے ہیں، لیکن آپ نے تو چھلکوں اور گٹھلیوں کو بھی نہیں چھوڑا۔

LESSON 14
TRANSLATION

(Translate into English)

Kitab par. Ādmī sē. Pānī meṅ. Dukān ko. khat meṅ. Topī par. Daftar ko. Sandūq sē. Aurat ko. Ghar meṅ. Kāghaz par. Naukar sē. Pēṭī meṅ. Chhurī se.

(Translate into Urdu)

To the women. In the house. On the paper. From the servant. On the water. In the letter. To the office. On the box. From the man. In the belt. To the shop.

(Translate into English)

Tum kaun ho? Main āpkā naukar hūṅ. Tumhārā ghar kahāṅ hai? Mērā ghar Delhi meṅ hai. Woh daftar meṅ hai. Ham dukān meṅ haiṅ. Āpkā naukar ghar meṅ hai. Woh daftar meṅ nahin hai. Woh mērā naukar hai. Tum kahāṅ ho? Main ghar meṅ hūṅ. Tum daftar meṅ nahin ho. Uskā ghar bāzār meṅ nahin hai.

(Translate into Urdu)

Who is he? He is my servant. I am in the office. They are not men. Where are you? He is in the office. We are in the shop. I am a washerman. Where is your house? He is not here. I am not his servant. They are not in the shop. He is not in my office. Which is your box?

163

(Translate into English)

Daftar ko aao. Ghar meṅ ṭhairo. Dukān ko jāo. Khat sandūq meṅ hai. Ṭopī mēz par hai. Mēz daftar sē lāo. Woh kāghaz sandūq meṅ rakho. Yeh sandūq ghar meṅ rakho.

(Translate into Urdu)

Come in the house. Go to the shop. Wait in the office. The hat is in the box. The letter is on the table. The table is in the shop. Bring the box to the shop. Put the paper in the box. Take (away) this book to the office. Send the hat to the house. Bring the stick from the house. Put the knife on the table. Wait on the verandah.

(Translate into English)
(I)

(۱) وہ زمین جو تمہارے بنگلے کے سامنے ہے اس کی قیمت کیا ہے؟ (۲) آج شام کولٹھ کے بغیر جنگل کے پار مت جاؤ۔ (۳) وہ ایک دوست کے ساتھ آج صبح یہاں تھا۔ (۴) اس بوڑھے آدمی کے لئے روٹی لاؤ۔ (۵) کل اس مہینے کا سب سے گرم دن تھا۔ (۶) وہ لڑکا جو باغ میں ہے میرے دوست کا سب سے بڑا بیٹا ہے۔ (۷) یہ خط کس کے لئے ہے؟ (۸) اس کی بابت آپ کی رائے کیا ہے؟ (۹) ممبئی ہندوستان کا سب سے بڑا شہر ہے۔ دہلی ہمارا سب سے زیادہ خوبصورت شہر ہے۔

۱۔ غسل خانہ کا دروازہ کس نے کھولا ہے۔ ۲۔ جب دھوبی کپڑے لایا تو نوکر نے دروازہ کھولا اور کپڑے صندوق میں رکھے۔ ۳۔ خزانے کے افسر نے اس کو چیک کا روپیہ نہیں دیا۔ ۴۔ میرے بیٹی نے سب پرانی کتابیں غریب لڑکے کو دے دیں۔ ۵۔ اس نے چوروں کو دیکھا۔ ۶۔ میں نہیں جانتا ہوں کہ اس نے یہ چٹھی میرے پاس کیوں بھیجی ہے۔ ۷۔ میں نے ایسا تماشہ کبھی نہیں دیکھا ہے۔ ۸۔ دھوبی نے قصائی کے گھر کا تالا توڑا۔ ۹۔ تم نے ہمارے کپڑے کلب کو کیوں نہیں بھیجے۔ ۱۰۔ اس سپاہی نے پولیس کو جھوٹی خبر بھیجی۔ ۱۱۔ چار آدمیوں نے بہت شراب پی، ایک دوکان کے اندر گئے اور اس کی سب کھڑکیاں توڑ دیں۔ ۱۲۔ بادشاہ نے ایک بہت اچھا گھوڑا اوز یر کو دے دیا ہے۔ ۱۳۔ گھوڑوں نے ابھی تک دانہ نہیں کھایا ہے۔ ۱۴۔ بدمعاش لڑکوں نے ڈاک گاڑی پر پتھر پھینکے۔ ۱۵۔ میں نہیں جانتا ہوں کہ اس نے میری جیب سے گھڑی کب اور کیسے نکالی۔ ۱۶۔ میں نے اس لڑکی کو پہلی مرتبہ گر جامیں دیکھا تھا۔

۱۔ ڈرپوک آدمی ہمیشہ مارتے کے آگے اور بھاگتے کے پیچھے ہوتا ہے۔ ۲۔ جب نوکر کتوں کو بھونکتے سن کر اپنے گھروں سے نکلے تو انہوں نے

چوروں کو بھاگتے دیکھا۔ ۳۔ میں نے آپ کو اس مدرسے میں جاتے ہوئے دیکھا۔ ۴۔ ہم نے ہوائی جہاز اڑتے ہوئے دیکھا۔ ۵۔ میں نے اس کو اردو بولتے کبھی نہیں سنا۔ ۶۔ ہم لوگ سرحد پر رہتے ہیں۔ ۷۔ اگر تم پڑوسیوں کی مرغیاں چراتے رہو گے تو تمہارے ہی لئے برا ہو گا۔ ۸۔ وہ بیوقوف آدمی ہمیشہ دوسروں کی بات میں دخل دیتا ہے۔ ۹۔ ہم جو کچھ کر سکتے ہیں کر رہے ہیں۔ ۱۰۔ کیا اس خط میں میرے لئے کوئی بات ہے؟ ۱۱۔ دروازے کے قریب آ کر یہ چیز رکھ لو۔ ۱۲۔ آپ کون ہیں اور کہاں رہتے ہیں؟ ۱۳۔ آپ کے والد (باپ) کا کیا نام ہے؟ ۱۴۔ آج کل آپ کی والدہ (ماں) کہاں رہتی ہیں؟ کیا وہ آپ کے ساتھ ہیں؟ ۱۵۔ جی ہاں، ہم سب لوگ اکٹھا ہی رہتے ہیں۔ ۱۶۔ جو صبح ہنستے اٹھتے ہیں وہ سارا دن خوش رہتے ہیں۔ ۱۷۔ اگر تم کو جانا ہی ہے تو پھر ابھی چلے جاؤ۔ ۱۸۔ کیا تم نے ریڈیو پر میری تقریر سنی تھی؟

(IV)

۱۔ لڑکے نے آپ اپنی گھڑی توڑی ہے۔ ۲۔ دیہاتی عورتیں اپنے گھر کا کام آپ کرتی ہیں۔ ۳۔ میرا سائیس آپ گھوڑے کے واسطے گھانس نہیں لائے گا۔ ۴۔ مولوی صاحب نے آج تم کو باغ میں دیکھا تھا۔ ۵۔ تم تیرنا جانتے ہو۔ ۶۔ بہادر آدمی مرنے اور مارنے سے نہیں ڈرتے ہیں۔

166

۷ـ ہر وقت ہنسنا اور دانت نکالنا بہت خراب عادتیں ہیں ـ ۸ ـ بات بنانا
آسان ہے لیکن کام کرنا بڑا مشکل ہے ـ ۹ ـ آپ کا نوکر آپ کو بلانے آیا
ہے ـ ۱۰ ـ تم یہاں سیکھنے کو آئے ہو یا سکھانے کو ـ ۱۱ ـ یہ دس روپے
تمہارے مٹھائی کھانے کو ہیں ـ ۱۲ ـ خدا نے دن کام کرنے کو اور رات
آرام کرنے کو بنائی ہے ـ ۱۳ ـ تمہاری عرضی جج صاحب کے سامنے رکھی
جائے گی ـ ۱۴ ـ ڈاکوؤں نے گھر کے اندر جا کر عورت سے پوچھا کہ تمہارا
زیور کہاں ہے اور یہ بھی کہا کہ اگر تم نہیں بتاؤ گی تو ہم تمہاری بچی کو
مار ڈالیں گے ـ ۱۵ ـ مالی سے کہو کہ بہت باتیں نہ بنائے اور جیسا حکم دیا گیا
ہے ویسا کرے ـ

(Read, write and translate into English)

(۱)

یہ ایک نواب کی کہانی ہے ـ ایک مرتبہ یہ نواب بیمار پڑا ـ حکیم کو بلا کر
تشخیص کروائی گئی ـ حکیم نے بتایا ـ ”جناب والا! آپ شیرینی کھانا
چھوڑ دیں ـ“

نواب نے کہا ”حکیم صاحب! بغیر شیرینی کے میری زندگی بیکار ہے ـ
اس لئے ہر روز صرف ایک لڈو کھانے کی اجازت دیجئے ـ“

نواب شیرینی کا بے حد شوقین تھا ـ آخر کار حکیم نے اسے آدھا لڈو

167

کھانے کی اجازت دے دی۔

''تب تو باقی آدھا لڈو آپ کو کھانا پڑیگا!'' نواب نے حکیم سے شرط لگائی۔

''ٹھیک ہے،ایسا ہی کرونگا۔'' حکیم نے اپنی رضامندی دے دی۔

دوسرے دن بارہ سیر وزن کا ایک لڈو نواب کے سامنے لایا گیا۔ حکیم بھی وہیں حاضر تھا۔ اس لڈو کو دیکھ کر حکیم کو بڑا تعجب ہوا۔

حکیم صاحب، آپ نے آدھا لڈو کھانے کی اجازت دی ہے۔ یہاں لڈو ہے اس میں آدھا میں کھاؤنگا اور باقی آدھا آپ کو کھانا ہے۔'' نواب نے حکیم سے کہا۔

(II)

بہت دنوں کی بات ہے۔ میسور کے نزدیک ایک گاؤں میں ایک بیوہ رہتی تھی۔ اس کا نام بھاگمّا کہا جاتا ہے۔ اس کے یہاں ایک مسلمان لڑکا نوکری کرتا تھا۔ اس کا نام حیدر تھا۔ بھاگمّا اسے اپنے لڑکے کی طرح پیار کرتی تھی۔ لڑکا حیدر بڑا ہوشیار اور بہادر تھا۔ وہ فوج میں داخل ہوگیا۔ دن بیتتے گئے۔ وہ اپنی محنت سے جلد ہی فوج کا سردار اور سردار سے میسور کا بادشاہ بن گیا۔

حیدر اب بادشاہ بن گیا لیکن اس بیوہ کو نہیں بھولا۔ ایک دن اپنے ساتھ قیمتی کپڑے، موتی، زیور وغیرہ لے کر ہاتھی پر سوار ہوا اور اس گاؤں کی طرف چل پڑا۔

یہ دیکھ کر وزیروں اور دوسرے نوکر چاکروں کو بڑا تعجب ہو رہا تھا۔ ہاتھی اس گاؤں میں پہنچا۔ بھاگتا کی اس جھونپڑی کے پاس آتے ہی بادشاہ ہاتھی سے اتر کر دروازہ کھٹکھٹانے لگا۔ اندر سے آواز آئی، کون ہے؟ بادشاہ حیدر نے بتایا۔ ''میں ہوں تمہارا پرانا نوکر حیدر۔'' بڑھیا بھاگتا دروازہ کھول کر باہر نکلی۔ اس کے منہ سے نکلا۔ ''بادشاہ!''

''ہاں ماں! تمہارا بیٹا۔ یہ نوکر تمہاری ہی دعاؤں سے آج بادشاہ بنا ہے۔ اسے اور دعائیں دو ماں۔'' بادشاہ حیدر نے اس کے پیروں کو چھوا اور لایا ہوا نذرانہ سامنے رکھا۔

بڑھیا نے بڑی خوشی کے ساتھ کہا۔ بیٹا یہ سب کیا ہے۔ تمہارے دل کی خوشی ہی میرے لئے قیمتی نذرانہ ہے۔ تم جگ جگ جیو بیٹا۔

(III)

اُن دنوں حاتم کا نام کون نہیں جانتا۔ وہ اپنی نیکی سے سب سے بڑا آدمی بن گیا تھا۔ لوگ اس کا بہت ادب کرتے۔ حاتم کے پاس بے شمار

دولت تھی ۔ وہ بہت سخی اور رحم دل تھا۔ ہمیشہ خیرات کیا کرتا تھا۔

ایک دن اس کے دوستوں میں سے ایک نے پوچھا۔ ''حاتم! کیا
تم نے کبھی اپنے سے زیادہ بڑے سخی اور رحم دل آدمی کو دیکھا ہے''۔

حاتم نے جواب دیا۔ ''ہاں دیکھا ہے''۔

''کہاں'' دوست نے پوچھا۔

حاتم نے بتایا۔ ''ایک دن میرے یہاں عام دعوت تھی۔ امیر
اور غریب سب آئے۔ اس دن شام کو میں جنگل کی طرف چلا۔ وہاں
ایک بوڑھا لکڑہارا سوکھی لکڑیاں جمع کر رہا تھا۔ میں نے اس سے پوچھا
کہ آج حاتم کے یہاں عام دعوت ہے۔ تم کیوں نہیں گئے؟

لکڑہارے نے جواب دیا۔ ''جب تک میرے ہاتھ پاؤں میں
طاقت ہے، کسی کے آگے ہاتھ کیوں پھیلاؤں''۔

اس کی یہ بات سن کر میری سمجھ میں آیا کہ میرے پاس دولت ہے۔
اس لئے دل بھی ہے۔ لیکن اس لکڑہارے کے پاس دولت بالکل نہیں ہے
پھر بھی وہ بہت بڑا دل والا ہے۔ اس لئے مجھ سے وہی بڑا ہے۔

(Translate into Urdu)

(1)

In those days who did not know the name of Hatim. He had become the greatest of all by his goodness. The people also were giving great respect to him. Hatim had innumerble riches. He was merciful. Always he used to give alms.

One day one of his friends asked him, "Hatim, have you ever seen any one greater than you?"

Hatim answered, "Yes, I have seen."

"Where?", the friend asked.

Hatim said, "One day there was a public feast in my house. The rich and poor all of them came. That day in the evening I went towards a forest. There was an aged wood-man collecting dry woods. I asked him, "There is a public feast in Hatim's house. Why didn't you go?"

The wood-man answered, "Why should I unfold my hands in front of (beg to) any one, as long as my hands and legs have strength."

Having heard this I came to know that I have riches, so I have heart too; but the woodman hasn't any riches, even then he has a great heart. So he is greater than me.

(II)

Some years ago an illiterate businessman who had to go to a certain city reached the Railway Station just as the train was about to depart. He asked the booking clerk for a ticket, but the latter said "I cannot issue a ticket to you as the train is just going." The businessman said, "Please give me a ticket, I must catch this train, else I shall suffer a great financial loss.

On hearing this the clerk gave him a ticket, and seizing it the businessman rushed off to catch the train. On reaching the train he found it was just starting. The businessman ran up the platform, and managed to get hold of a door handle and stand on the footboard. But to his annoyance a Railway policeman caught him by the arm and pulled him off the train, saying to him, "No one is allowed to get into a moving train."

Just then the businessman saw the gurard, getting into the guard's van. He ran and seizing the guard by the arm, pulled him off. On being asked by the irate guard why he pulled him off, the businessman told him that a Railway policeman had just told him that no one is allowed to get into a moving train.

(III)

A king had a jester, who always used to chew tobacco. Consequently his breath was always very unpleasant. The king did not like this and several times forbade him to chew tobacco, but the jester would not give up this habit. As he was such a good jester, the king did not want to dismiss him.

It so happened that one day the king went out shooting accompained as usual by his jester. The royal camp was pitched near some tobacco fields. There were some donkeys grazing in these fields, and the king noticed that they only ate the grass, leaving the tobacco aside.

The king at once called for his jester, and pointing to the donkeys said to him, "Look! even the donkeys do not eat tobacco."

"Your Majesty is quite right, donkeys do not eat tobacco", answered the jester smilingly.

(Translate into Urdu)

(I)

1. I shall not go to the club today. 2. Will your brother read this book? 3. When will the coolie arrive here? 4. I shall send two servants with you. 5. The Major will not come to the office today. 6. Who will give you two thousand rupees for this lame horse? 7. He will not give you any advance. 8. I shall be ready presently. 9. I know that you will not make such a mistake again. 10. Will you

also go with my brother for shooting? 11. His wife will not go with him to the dance. 12. Two mares will also run in the race. 13. I will beat your son, if I see him again in this room.

(II)

1. The ripest fruit falls first (of all). 2. Whom are you calling? 3. I do not eat meat often. 4. I am looking for my hat, which I put on this table an hour ago. 5. Why have you not got up yet? 6. What were you doing with that knife? 7. Do you not see what I am doing? 8.Who is this gentleman, who is coming towards us? 9. Where is the envelope on which you wrote the address just now? 10. I am going home, will you come with me? 11. What did you do during the holidays? 12. Somebody is calling you. 13. This is not the stick, which I left in that corner; some one has changed it. 14. If you had told the waiter, he would have brought two bottles of beer, one for you and one for me. 15. I do not know why he has not sent the answer to my letter yet. 16. If you see the dog in the garden, send it back to its owner. 17. If the doctor had come here, I would have shown him the wound. 18. I have heard that he will not do it. 19. If I had given even five hundred rupees to my servant, he would have spent them all in one day. 20. What are you thinking about? 21. I heard all what he said. 22. He may not arrive here by ten. 23. I will give the children all the fruits and flowers, which I brought from the jungle.

(III)

Delhi is the capital of India. It is an old city and till now we can see the remains of very antique times. This is such a beautiful city that once one comes in he never thinks of leaving it to settle elsewhere. In the culture of this city there is some such thing that we are forced to say—Leaving away Delhi's streets, Ghalib, where else you will go?

(IV)

Books are strange gifts. When in our lives hover the dark clouds of distress, then books like true friends provide us consolation. When other dear friends and relatives leave us in ill times, books stick to us. They increase our courage and teach us how to win over difficulties. Books are the result of man's continuous work of thousands of years. Even then all books are not good. We should choose only good books for reading.

(V)

In man's life, childhood is the best of times. In this age there is no worry, parents and other people show love, give good things to eat and good clothes to wear and as far as possible provide for full comfort even though they have to bear difficulties for this. For their children some parents break stones, some carry loads, even then whatever is possible is done so that the progeny can live in comfort.

175

VOCABULARY
ENGLISH – URDU

Abbreviations

m. Masculine, *f.* Feminine, *adj.* Adjective, *adv.* Adverb, *c.* Conjunction, *In.* Interjection. *Pro.* Pronoun, *Pre.* Preposition, *v. tr.* Verb Transitive. *v. int.* Verb Intransitive, *k.* karna; *h* hona; *d.* dena; *j.* jana.

A

Abandon	Chhor denā	Abundant	Bahut.
Ability	liāqat *f.*	Abuse	Gāli *f.*
Able *adj.*	Lāiq.	Abuse *v. tr.*	Gāli denā.
Abode	Ṭhikāna *m.*	Accept	Qabūl karnā.
Abolish	Mauqūf karnā	Access	Pahunch *f.*
Abound	Kasrat se honā	Accident	Hādisā *m.*
About *(nearly)*	Taqrīban.	Accordingly	Chunācheh.
About (Concerning)	ki bābat.	According to	Ke muāfiq
		Accurate	Theek
Above	Ke upar.	Accusation	ilzām *m.*
Abreast	Barābar.	Accuse	(par) ilzām lagānā
Abroad	Pardes *m.*		
Abruptly *abv.*	Eka eki.	Accused	Mulzim
Absent *adj.*	Ghair hāzir.	Across	Ke pār
Absence *adj.*	Ghair hāziri.	Active	Chust, sargram
Absolute *adj.*	Mutlaq.	Actual *adj.*	Asl
Absurd *adj.*	Behūda.	Address	Pata
Abundance	Kasrat *f.*	Admiration	Tārif *f.*

Admonish to	Tañbih *k.*	Ascend	Charhnā
Advance (money)	Peshgi *f.*	Ascent	Charhāi *f.*
		Ascertain	Tahqeeq *k.*
Appoint *v. tr.*	Muqarrar karnā	Ashamed *adj.*	Sharminda
Apprehend, to	Giriftār karnā	Ashes	Rakh
Approval	Manzūri *f.*	Ask	Puchhnā
Approve	Manzūr karna	Ask for	Mañgnā
Approximately	Andāzan.	Ass	Gadhā
Area	Raqba; Ilāqah	Assist	(ko) Madad denā
Argue	Hujjat *k. v. tr.*		
Arm	Bāzū.	Assist	(ki) Madad karnā
Armed *adj.*	Hathyār band.		
Armpit	Baghal *f.*	Assure	(ko) Yaqin dilanā
Arms	Hathyār		
Army	Fauj *f.*	Attach	Lagānā
Arrange, to	Band-o-bast *k.*	Attack	(par) Hamla *k.*
Arrangement	Band-o-bast.	Attempt	Koshish karna
Arrears	Bāqi *f.*	Auction	Nilām *m.*
Arrest	Giriftar	Authority	Ikhtiar
Arrest, to be under	Hawālāt meñ honā.	Avarice	Lālach *m.*
		Avaricious *adj.*	Lālchi
Arrive	Pahuñchnā	Average	Ausat *f.*
Arsenal	Aslah khāna	Awkward	Bhunda
Art	Hunar *m.*	Axe	Kulhāri
Artful	Chālbāz.	Axle	Dhura
Artillery	Topkhāna *m.*		

B

Back	Peeth *f.*	Backwards *adv.*	Peechhe
Back *adv.*	Wāpas.	Bag	Thaili *f.*

177

Baggage	Asbab *m.*	Beat, to	Mārnā
Bail	Zamanat *f.*	Beautiful	Khūbsūrat *f.*
Bald	Ganja	Beauty	Khūbsūrtī *f.*
Bamboo	Bāñs *m.*	Because	Kioñkeh *c.*
Banana	Kēlā *m.*	Bedding	Bistar *m.*
Bandage	Paṭṭī *f.*	Beef	Gāe kā gosht *m.*
Bank; shore	Kināra *m.*	Before	Sē pahlē or kē
Banker	Sarrāf *m.*		sāmnē
Banner	Jhanda *m.*	Beggar	Faqir *m.*
Barber	Nai, hajjām *m.*	Begin	Shurū *k.*
Bare (naked)	Nañgā	Behaviour	Chāl chalan
Bargain	Saudā *m.*	Behind	Kē pichhē
Bark of a tree	Chhāl *f.*	Believe, to	Yaqin *k.*
Bark, to	Bhauñknā	Bell	Ghanṭi
Barley	Jau *m.*	Belly	Pēṭ *m.*
Barrel (gun)	Nālī *f.*	Belt	Peṭī *f.*
Base (mean)	Kamīna	Bend	Jhuknā; morna
Basket	Ṭokra *m.* or	Benefit	Fāeda *m.*
	Tokrī *f.*	Besides	Kē alāwa
Bath	Ghusl *m.*	Besiege	Ghērnā
Bathe	Nahānā	Bet	Shart *f.*
Battle	Larāī *f.*	Better	Behtar
Bayonet	Sangin *f.*	Between	Kē darmiān
Be, to	Honā	Beyond	Kē parē; bāhar
Beak	Choñch *f.*	Bier	Janāza *m.*
Bear *v.t.*	Uthānā	Bill (account)	Hisāb *m.*
Bear	Bhālu; reechh *m.*	Bird	Parinda
Beard	Dārhī *f.*	Bitch	Kutiā *f.*
Beast	Jānwar *m.*	Bite	Kāṭnā

Bitter	Karwā	Boyhood	Larakpan
Blacksmith	Lūhār m.	Brain	Bheja, Damagh
Blank (paper)	Sādā	Bran	Chokar, Bhusi
Blind	Andhā	Branch	Shākh
Blood	Khūn, lahu m.	Brass	Pital
Blue	Nila	Brave	Bahādur
Blunt	Kund	Bravery	Bahaduri
Board	Takhta m.	Bread	Roti f.
Boast v. tr.	Shēkhī mārnā	Break	Tornā
Boat	Kishti f.	Breakfast	Nashta; hāzri
Body	Badan, jism m.	Breast	Chhāti
Body (dead)	Lāsh f.	Breath	Dam; sāns
Boil	Phorā m.	Bribe	Rishwat
Boil v. int.	Khulnā	Brick	Eint f.
Boil v. tr.	Khulānā	Bridge	Pul m.
Bold	Dilare	Bright	Raushan
Bone	Haddi f.	Bring	Lānā
Booty	Loot kā maal	Bring up	Pālnā
Border	Kināra	Broken	Tūtā hūā.
Born (to be)	Paidā honā	Broom	Jhāru f.
Borrow	Qarz lēnā	Brother	Bhāi
Bosom	Sina m.	Buck	Hiran m.
Both	Donoñ	Bucket	Bālti f.
Bough	Shākh	Buffalo	Bhains f.
Boundless	Be-had	Build	Banānā
Boundary	Had f.	Bullet	Goli f.
Bouquet	Guldasta m.	Bullock	Bail m.
Box	Sandūq	Bunch	Guch-chhā.
Boy	Larkā	Bundle	Gathri f.

Burn v. tr.	Jalānā	Business	Kām;
Burn v. Int.	Jalnā		Kar-o-bar m.
Burden	Bojh	But	Lēkin
Burst	Phatnā	Butt	Kunda m.
Bury	Dabānā	Butcher	Qasāi
Bush	Jhāri f.	Buy	Kharidnā

C

Cage	pinjra m.	Care, to take	Khabardār
Calamity	Āfat f.		honā.
Calculate	Hisāb lagānā m.	Carefully	Hushyāri se
Calculation	Hisāb	Careless	Beparwah
Call, to	Bulānā	Carpenter	Barhai m.
Camel	Ūnt m.	Carriage	Gāṛi f.
Camp	Parāo	Carry	Lejānā
Campaign	Larāi f. lām m.	Cartridge	Kārtūs m.
Camphor	Kāfūr. m.	Case (law)	Muqaddama.
Canal	Nahr f.	Case (condition)	Hāl.
Candle	Mombatti f.	Cash	Naqd m.
Cane	Baid	Caste	Zāt f.
Cannon	Top f.	Casualty	Nuqsan (Murde
Cantonment	Chhāoni f.		aur Zakhmi)
Cap	Ṭopi	Cat	Billī
Capital (town)	Dārul Hukumat	Catch	Pakaṛnā
Capture	Pakaṛnā	Cause	Sabab m.
Caravan	Qāfla m.	Cavalry	Risāla.
Care	Fikr; parwah	Cave	Ghaar

Cease fire, to	Golabari band *k.*	Clock	Gharee
Ceiling	Chhat *f.*	Cloth	Kaprā *m.*
Centre	Bich/Markaz *m.*	Cold, cool	Thandā
Century	Sadi *f.*	Collect	Jama karnā
Ceremony	Rasm; Taqreeb *f.*	Commence	Shurū *k.*
Certainly	Zarūr, Beshak.	Common	Aam, m'amuli
Chain	Zanjeer	Commonly	Amūman
Chair	Kursi	Complain, to	Shikāyat *k.*
Chance	Ittefāq	Complete	Pūra.
Change, to	Badalnā	Compound	Ehata *m.*
Charcoal	Koelā	Comrade	Sāthi *m.*
Cheap	Sastā	Conceal	Chhupānā
Cheat, to	Thagnā	Condition	Hālat
Cheese	Paniar *m.*	Confidently	Itminān se
Chew	Chabānā.	Consent	Marzi *f.*
Child	Bachcha *m.*	Consider	Sochnā
Chin	Thori *f.*	Contagious	Phailne wala
Cholera	Haiza *m.*	Continually	Barābar;
Choose	Pasand *k.*		musalsal
Church	Girjā *m.*	Contract	Theka *m.*
Circle	Ghera *m.*	Contractor	Thekedar
City	Shahr *m.*	Copy *v. tr.*	Naql *k.*
Claim	Dawā *m.*	Cord	Dori *f.*
Class	Darja	Corner	Kona *m.*
Clean, clear	Saaf	Correct	Theek
Clever	Hushyār	Country (Rural)	Dehāt
Cleverly	Hushyāri se	Cover *v. tr.*	Dhaknā
Climb	Charhnā	Covetous	Lālchi
Clip, to	Kātnā	Cow	Gāe *f.*

Coward	Buzdil; darpok	Cruelty	Zulm
Cowherd	Goālā; charwāhā	Cry v. Int.	Ronā, chillanā.
Cream	Malāī f.	Culprit	Mujrim m.
Crew	Jahāzī	Cultivation	Khetī f.
Crime	Jurm m.	Cultivator	Kisān
Crooked	Ṭerhā adj.	Cup	Piāla m.
Crop	Fasl f.	Cunning	Chālak
Cross	Ke pār jānā	Cure v. tr.	Ilaaj k.
Cross-road	Churāha m.	Curtain	Parda m.
Crow	Kawwā m.	Curve	Mor m.
Crowd	Hujūm	Cushion	Gaddi f.
Crown	Tāj m.	Custom	Dastūr; Rasm
Cruel	Zālim.	Customs	Mahsūl m.

D

Dacoit	Dāku	Daughter	Betī
Daily	Rozaana	Dawn adv.	Din nikle; subha tarke
Damage	Nuqsān m.		
Damage v. tr.	Nuqsān k.	Day	Din or roz m.
Damp	Namdār.	Day by Day	Roz-ba-roz
Dance	Nāch m.	Dead of night	Aadhī raat
Dance v. tr.	Nāchnā	Deaf adj.	Bahrā
Danger	Ḍar, khatra m.	Dealing	Len den m.
Dangerous adj.	Khatrnak	Dear (expensive)	
Dark	Andhērā		Mahṅgā
Date	Tārīkh f.	Deduct v. tr.	Kātnā
Date (fruit)	Khajūr m.	Deep	Gahrā

Deface v. tr.	Kharab k.	Defile v. tr.	Ganda k.
Defeat	Shikast f.	Delay v. tr.	Der k.
Defeat v. tr.	Shikast d.	Delicate	Nazuk
Defeated,		Delight	Khushi
to be	Shikast khana	Delicious	Mazedar
Defect	'Aieb' m.	Demand v. tr.	Mangna
Defective	'Aiebdar	Demolish v. tr.	Ujarna
Defence	Bachao m.	Denial	Inkar m.
Defend	Bachana	Deny v. tr.	(se) Inkar k.
Deficient	Kam		

E

Each	Har ek	Enquiry	Tahqiqat,
Ear	Kan		pochh-guchh
Early	Jaldi	Enter	Dakhil h.
Early in the	Subah sawere	Entirely	Bilkul
morning		Entrench	Morcha
Earn v. tr.	Kamana		banana
Earth (ground)	Zameen f.	Envelope	Lifafa m.
Earth (world)	Dunya	Equal adj.	Barabar
(ground)	Zameen f.	Erase v. tr.	Mitana
Earthquake	Bhaunchal m.	Erect v. tr.	Khara k.
Ease	Aaram	Exertion	Mehnat f.
East	Mashriq f.	Expenditure	Kharch m.
Education	Taleem	Expensive adj.	Mehnga
Effects	Asbab; maal	Explain v. tr.	Samjhana
Effort	Koshish f.	Explanation	Bayan m.
Enmity	Dushmani		Jawab m.
Enough	Kafi	Extinguish v. tr.	Bujhana
		Eye	Aankh f.

F

Face	Muñh; chehra *m.*	Fill *v. tr.*	Bharnā
Fact	Asl bāt *f.*	Filth	Kūrā
Fair (show)	Mēla	Find *v. tr.*	Pānā
Fair *adj.*	Khāsa	Fine (money)	Jurmānā *m.*
Faithful	Wafādār	Fine *v. tr.*	(par)
Falsehood	Jhūṭ		Jrmānā *k.*
Family	Kunba *m.*	Fine *adj.*	Umda
Famous	Mashhūr	Finger	Uñglī
Fare	Kirāya *m.*	Finish *v. tr.*	Khatm *k.*
Farrier	Nāl band *m.*	Finish *v. int.*	Khatm *h.*
Fat *adj.*	Moṭā	Fire	Aag *f.*
Fate	Qismat *f.*	First	Pahlā
Fatigue	Thakān	Flag (big)	Jhanḍā *m.*
Fault	Qasūr *m.*	(small)	Jhanḍi *f.*
Favour	Mehrbānī	Floor	Farsh *m.*
Fear	Ḍar *m.*	Flow	Bahnā
Fear *v. Int.*	Ḍarnā	Flower	Phūl *m.*
Feed *v. tr.*	Khilānā	Fly, to	Urnā
Felt	Namda *m.*	Foolishness	Bewaqūfī
Female	Māda *f.*	Foot of hill	Pahar kā
Fight, to	Larnā		dāman

G

Game	Shikār *m.*	Gather *v. tr.*	Jama *k.*
Game (play)	Khel	Gather *v. int.*	Jama *h.*
Garden	Bāgh	Generally	Umuman
Gate	Phāṭak	Gently	Āhista se

184

Girth	Ghaira f.	Gratuity	In 'ām f.
Glad adj.	Khūsh	Grave	Qabr f.
Glove	Dastāna m.	Graze	Charnā
Goat	Bakrā m.	Green adj.	Harā
God	Khudā m.	Grief	Ranj m.
Gold	Sonā m.	Groom v. tr.	Mālish k.
Goodness	Bhalāī, nēkī f.	Ground	Zamin f.
Goods	Maal m.	Groundless adj.	Be bunyād
Govern v. tr.	Hukūmat k.	Grow	Ugnā
Grain	Dāna m.	Guardian	Muhāfiz
Grape	Angūr m.	Guest	Mehmān m.
Grass	Ghāñs	Guess v. tr.	Qayas k.
Gratis	Muft		

H

Habit	Aadat f.	Handle	Dasta m.
Hair	Baal	Hang v. tr. (suspend)	Latkānā
Half adj.	Aadha.		
Halt	Parao m.	Hang v. tr. (execute)	(ko) Phañsi d.
Handkerchief	Rumal m.		
Heap	Dher m.	Honesty	Imāndāri
Hear, to	Sunnā	Honour	Izzat
Heart	Dil m.	Hoof	Sum; Khur m.
Heat	Garmi f.	Hope	Ummeed
Heaven	Bahisht f.	Host	Mēzbān
Heavy adj.	Bhāri	However	Magar

I

Ice	Barf f.	Idea	Khyāl m.

185

Idle *adj.*	Sust	Inkpot	Dawāt
Ignorant	Jāhil, nādān	Inn	Sarāe *f.*
Important *adj.*	Zarūri	Instalment	Qist *f.*
Impossible *adj.*	Nā mumkin	Instead of	Ke badle
Inhabitant	Bashinda *m.*	Insufficient	Nā kāfi
Injure *v. tr.*	Nuqsān *k.*	Insult *v. tr.*	Be-izzati *k.*
Injustice	Be-Insāfi *f.*	In vain *adv.*	Befāeda
Ink	Siāhi *f.*	Invasion	Hamla *m.*

J

Jackal	Gidar *m.*	Joint *n.*	Jor
Jaw	Jabrā *m.*	Joke *v. tr.*	Mazāq *k.*
Jealous *adj.*	Hāsid	Journey	Safar *m.*
Jerk *v. tr.*	Jhatkā mārnā	Joy	Khūshi *f.*

K

Keen	Shauqin	Kindly	Mehrbāni se
Keep	Rakhnā	King	Bādshāh
Kettle	Ketli *f.*	Kingdom	Bādshāhat
Key	Chābi *f.*	Kitchen	Bāwarchi
Kick (man)	Thokar mārnā		khāna *m.*
Kick *v. tr.*	Lāt mārnā		
(of horse)		Kite (bird)	Cheel *f.*
Kill	Mar dalnā	Knee	Ghutna *m.*
Killed	Mar jānā	Know	Jānnā
Kindness	Mehrbāni *f.*	Knowledge	Ilm *m.*

L

Land	Zamīn	Light *adj.*	Halka
Language	Zabān *f.*	Light *v. tr.*	Jalānā
Law	Qanūn	Like *v. tr.*	Pasand karna
Leaf	Patta *m.*	Like *adv.*	Ki tarah
Learn *v. tr.*	Sikhnā	Likewise	Is hi tarah
Leather	Chamrā *m.*	Limit	Had *f.*
Leave	Chhuttī *f.*	List	Fehrist
Leave *v. tr.*	Chhornā	To live (dwell) *v. int.* Rahna	
Left	Bāyāṅ	To live (exist) *v. int.* Jeena	
Leg	Taaṅg *f.*	Load	Bojh *m.*
Leisure	Fursat *f.*	Load *v. tr.*	Lādnā
Lend	Qarz dēnā	Lock, to	Tāla lagānā
Less	Kam	Look	Dēkhnā
Lesson	Sabaq	Look for	Talāsh *k.*
Letter	Chitthī *f.*	Loose *adj.*	Dheelā
Lick *v. tr.*	Chātnā	Lose *v. tr.*	Khonā
Lie (animate)	Lētnā	Lose (a bet) *v. tr.* Hārnā	
Lie (inanimate)	Parnā	Loss	Nuqsān
Life	Jān *f.*	Luck	Qismat *f.*
Light	Roshnī *f.*		

M

Mad *adj.*	Pāgal	Mark	Nishān *m.*
Mail train	Dāk gārī *f.*	Marriage	Shādī *f.*
Mango tree	Ām kā darakht	Marry *v. tr.*	Se shādi *k.*
Manner	Tariqa *m.*	Master (owner)	Malik
March *v. tr.*	Kūch karnā	Matter	M'uāmlā *m.*

Measure *v. tr.*	Nāpnā	Necessity	Zarurat
Meat	Gosht *m.*	Misfortune	Musibat *f.*
Medal	Tamgha *m.*	Missing	Kam, ghaib
Meddle	Dakhl dēnā	Mistake	Ghalati *f.*
Medical	Dāktar kā or	Mix *v. tr.*	Milānā
	Tib-bi	Money (ready)	Naqd *m.*
Medicine	Dawā *f.*	Monkey	Bandar *m.*
Mend *v. tr.*	Marammat *k.*	Month	Mahina
Merchant	Saudāgar or	Moon	Chānd *m.*
	Tājir	Mount *v. tr.*	Charhnā
Message	Paighām *m.*	Mountain	Pahār
Method	Tariqa *m.*	Mouth	Munh *m.*
Middle	Beech; wast	Mud	Kichar
Mile	Meel *f.*	Muddy *adj.*	Gadlā
Military	Fauj *f.*	Mule	Khachchar *m.*
Mind	Zahen *m.*	Murder	Qatl *k.*
Mischief	Sharārat *f.*	Mosquito	Machchhar *m.*
Miserly *adj.*	Kanjūs *f.*	Mutiny	Ghadar *m.*

N

Nail	Keel *f.*	Neck	Gardan *f.*
Nail (of finger)	Nākhun *m.*	Neglect *v. tr.*	Ghaflat *k.*
Naked *adj.*	Nangā	Neighbour	Parausi *m.*
Narrow *adj.*	Tang	Neighbourhood	Paraus *m.*
Nation	Qaum *f.*	Net	Jaal *m.*
Native *adj.*	Dēsi	News	Khabar *f.*
Navy	Behri Fouj *m.*	Noble *adj.*	Sharif
Necessary *adj.*	Zarūri *f.*	Noise	Shor *m.*

Nonsense	Wāhiāt f.	Now and then	Kabhī kabhī
Noon	Do pahar	Nuisance	Wabāl m.
North	Shumāl m.	Number	Gintī. f.
Nose	Nāk f.		tedād f.
Nowadays	Aaj kal	Numerous adj.	Beshumār

O

Oath (to take an) v. tr.		Ordinary	Māmūlī
	Qasm khānā	Opinion	Rāe f.
Obey v. Int.	(hukm) Mānnā	Opportunity	Mauqa m.
Object	Matlab m.	Opposite	Sāmne
Object v. tr.	Etrāz k.	Oppress v. tr.	Satānā
Oblique	Terhā; Tirchhā	Oral	Zabānī
Obtain	Hāsil k.	Order (method)	Tartīb
Occasion	Mauqa m.	Order	
Occupation	Pēsha m.	(command)	hukm
Offend, to v. tr.	Nārāz k.	Orderly	Ardalī m.
Official adj.	Sarkārī	Original	Asl
Often adv.	Aksar	Ornament	Zewar m.
Old age	Burhāpā	Otherwise	Warnah
Once	Ēk dafa	Outward	Bāhar kī taraf
Only	Sirf	Owner	Malik m.
Open, to	Kholnā	Ox	Bail m.
Openly adv.	Zahir men		

P

Pace	Qadam m.	Pain	Dard
Pack v. tr.	Bāndhnā	Parade	Qawāid, pared
Page	Safha m.	Pardon, to v. tr.	Mu'āf k.

Parents	Man bap	Particularly *adj.*	Khaskar ke
Part	Hissa *m.*	Peacock	Mor *m.*
Particular *adj.*	Khaskar	People (plural)	Log.

Q

Quail	Batair	Question *v. tr.*	Sawal *k.*
Quarrel	Jhagra *m.*	Quickly	Jaldi se
Quarrel *v. int.*	Jhagarna	Quietly	Chupke se
Queen	Maleka *f.*	Quite *adv.*	Bilkul
Queer *adj.*	'Ajeeb		

R

Rebel *v. tr.*	Baghawat	Remember *v.tr.*	Yad *k.*
Receipt	Rasid	Remind *v. tr.*	(ko) Yad dilana
Recently	Hal hi men	Rent	Kiraya
Recognize *v. tr.*	Pahchanna	Repairs	Marammat *f.*
		Repair *v. tr.*	ki Marammat *k.*
Recommend *v.tr.*	Sifarish *k.*	Rope	Rassi *f.*
		Rotten *adj.*	Sara hua
Recruit	Rangrut	Round *adj.*	Gol
Refuse *v. tr.*	(se) Inkar *k.*	Row (a line)	Qatar *f.*
Regiment	Paltan *f.*	Royal	Shahi
Regret *v. Int.*	Pachhtana	Rub *v. tr.*	Malna
Reins	Baag; lagam *f.*	Reward *v. tr.*	In 'am *d.*
Relation	Rishta *m.*	Rice	Chawal *m.*
Relative	Rishtedar	Ride *v. tr.*	Sawar *h.*
Release *v. tr.*	Chhorna	Riches	Daulat *f.*
Religion	Mazhab *m.*	Rifle	Raifal *f.*

190

Right (Proper)	Theek	Robbery	Daka
Right *adj.*	Dayan or	Rock	Chatan *f.*
(not left)	Dahna	Roof	Chhat *f.*
Ripe *adj.*	Pakka	Root	Jar *f.*
Rise *v. Int.*	Uthna; Nikalna	Rubbish	Kura *m.*
River	Darya *m.*	Ruin *v. tr.*	Barbad *k.*
Road Metalled	Sarak	Rule	Qaeda *m.*
Roar	Dhar *f.*	Rush	Jhapatna
Rob *v. tr.*	Lutna.	Rust	Zang *m.*
Robber	Daku *m.*		

S

Saddle	Zeen	Silent *adj.*	Chup
Safe *adj.*	Salamat, mahfuz	Silk	Resham
		Silver	Chandi *f.*
Safety	Hifazat	Sin	Gunah *m.*
Salt	Namak *m.*	Sing *v. Int.*	Gana
Salutation	Salam *m.*	Single file	Ek qatar
Salute *v. tr.*	Ko salam *k.*	Sink	Dubna
Same	Woh hi; ek hi	Sister	Bahen
Side	Taraf *f.*	Sit	Baithna
Side (of person)	Pahlu *m.*	Skilful *adj.*	Hushyar
Seize *v. tr.*	Pakarna	Skin	Khal *f.*
Sight show	Tamasha	Sky	Asman *m.*
Sign *v. tr.*	Ishara *k.*	Slave	Ghulum *m.*
Sign *v. tr.* (a paper)	(par) Dastkhat *k.*	Sleep	Neend *f.*
		Sleep, to	Sona
Signature	Dastkhat *m.*	Sleeve	Aasteen
Silence	Khamoshi *f.*	Slip *v. int.*	Phisalna

Slow	Dhimā; ahista
Smell v. tr.	Sunghnā
Smoke	Dhuāṅ m.
Send	Bhaijnā
Send (for thing)	Maṅgwānā
Sense	Hosh m.
Senseless	Behosh
Separate v. tr.	Judā k.
Separately adv.	Judā Judā
Serve v. tr.	Naukri k.
Some	Kuchh
Sometimes	Kabhi Kabhi
Somewhere	Kahiṅ
Sorrow	Afsos
Sort	Qism f.
Soup	Shorbā m.
South	Junūb.
Spare adj.	Faltū
Special	Khās
Speed	Raftaar f.
Spend v. tr.	Kharch k.
Spit v. tr.	Thūknā
Spoil v. tr.	Bigārnā; barbād karnā
Spoon	Chamcha m.
Spread v. tr.	Phailānā
Spread v. int.	Phailnā
Spy	Jāsus m.
Squander v. tr.	Dhaae k. Barbād k.
Stable	Astabal m.
Stale adj.	Bāsi
Stand int.	Kharā h.
Start	Rawāna hona
Statement	Bayān m.
Steal v. tr.	Churānā
Step	Qadam
Step out, to	Qadam barhānā
Stone	Patthar m.
Stop	Roknā
Storm	Tufān
Storm (wind)	Andhi
Story	Kahāni f.
Storey (of house)	Manzil f.
Straight adj.	Sidha
Stranger	Ajnabi m.
Strap	Tasma m.
Stream	Nadi f.
Strength	Taaqat f.
Strike	Mārnā
Student	Talib-e-ilm
Submarine	Aab doz
Success	Kamyabi
Successful	Kamyab h.

Such	Aisā	Suspiciously	Shak ke sāth
Summer	Garma f.	Sweet	Mithai
Sun	Sūraj m.	Sword	Talwar f.
Sunshine	Dhūp	Sympathy	Hamdardi f.

T

Tail	Dum	Thorn	Kāntā m.
Tall	Lambā	Thought	Khiāl
Take	Lēnā	Thousand	Hazār
Take off	Utārnā	Threaten v. tr.	Dhamki d.
Take out	Nikālnā	Throat	Galā
Tank	Talaab m.	Throw v. tr.	Phēnknā
Tape	Feeta m.	Thumb	Angūthā m.
Target	Nishāna	Thunder	Garaj f.
Teach v. tr.	Sikhānā	Thus adv.	Is tarah
Telegram	Taar m.	Tiger	Shēr
Temper	Mizāj m.	Tie v. tr.	Bāndhnā
Temporary adj.	Aardhi	Tigress	Shērni
Tent	Dēra; tambu	Tight adj.	Tang
Terrible	Khaufnāk	Time	Waqt
Theft	Chori	Time (leisure)	Fursat f.
Therefore	Is wāstē; Is lie	Tongue	Zabān f.
Thick adj.	Mota	Tooth	Dānt m.
Thigh	Rān; jāngh f.	Top of hill	Pahar ki choti
Thin, lean	Dublā, Patlā m.	Torment	Satana
Thing	Cheez f.	Touch v. tr.	Chhuna
Think v. tr.	Sochna	Tour	Daura m.
Thirsty	Piasa	Towards	Ki taraf

193

Towel	Taulia *m.*	Tribe	Qabila *m.*
Tower	Burj *m.*	Trick	Chāl *f.*
Transport	Bārbardāri	Trouble	Taklif *f.*
Travel *v. tr.*	Safar	Trousers	Patlūn or
Treasury	Khazānā		Pāejāma
Traveller	Musāfir	Try *v. tr.*	Koshish *k.*
Treat *v. tr.*	Salūk *k.*	Tunnel	Surang
Treatment	Ilaaj	Turn	Ghumānā
(Medical)		Tyranny	Zulm *m.*
Tremble *v. Int.*	Kāńpnā, larzna	Tyrant	Zalim
Trench	Morcha		

U

Ugly	Badsūrat	Unreasonable	Bejā
Unaware	Bekhabar	Unsafe	Ghair mahfooz
Unconscious	Behosh	Unusual	Ghair māmūli
Understand	Samajhnā	Upper	Upar kā
Undoubtedly	Beshak	Urgent *adj.*	Fouri
Unfit *adj.*	Naqabil	Urine	Peshāb
Unfortunately	Bad qismati se	Use(benefit)	Fāeda
Uniform	Wardi *f.*	Use *v. tr.*	Istemāl *k.*
Union	Anjuman *f.*	Useless	Befāeda
Unintentionally	Nadānista	Usual *adv.*	Mamūli
Unopposed	Be rok tok	Usually	Amūman
Unpleasant	Nāgawār	Utensil	Bartan *m.*

V

Vacant *adj.*	Khali	Value	Qīmat
Vaccinate	Tika lagānā	Valuable *adj.*	Qīmti

Vegetables	Tarkāri	Vinegar	Sirka *m.*
Verbal	Zabāni	Virtue	Nēki *f.*
Verification	Tasdiq *f.*	Voice	Āważ *f.*
Vicious	Badkar	Vomit *v. tr.*	Qae *k.*
Victory	Fatah, Jit *f.*	Vow	Ahd *m.*
Victorious	Fatehmand	Vulture	Gidh
Village	Gāoṅ *m.*		

W

Waist	Kamar *f.*	Wherever	Jahāṅ kahiṅ
Wall	Diwār *f.*	Wheel	Pahiya *m.*
War	Larāi *f.*	Whip	Chābuk *m.*
Warn	Taṅbih	Whistle *v. tr.*	Siti bajāna
Wash *v. tr.*	Dhonā	Whistle *f.*	Siti
Waste *v. tr.*	Barbād *k.*	White	Safaid
Weapon	Hathiār *m.*	Whole	Sab; Tamam
Weather	Mausam *m.*	Wick *f.*	Batti
Wedding	Shādi *f.*	Wicked	Badmāsh
Weight *v. tr.*	Tolnā	Widow	Bewa
Weight	Wazan *m.*	Width	Chaurāi *f.*
Well	Kuāṅ *m.*	Wife	Biwi
Well *adj.*	Tandurust	Wild	Jaṅgli
Well-known *adj.*	Maeroof	Wilfully	Jān būjh kar
		Willingly *adj.*	Khūshi sē
West	Maghrib	Win *v. tr.*	Jeetna
Whatever	Jo kuchh	Wind	Hawā *f.*
Whenever	Jab kabhi	Winding	Mordār
		Window	Khirki *f.*

Wine	Sharāb	Woolen *adj.*	Ūnī
Wing	Bāzū *m.*	Word	Lafz *m.*
Winter	Jāṛā *m.*	Work	Kām
Wipe *v. tr.*	Poñchhna	World	Dunyā *f.*
Wire	Tār *m.*	Wound	Zakhm *m.*
Wisdom	Aql *f.*	Wounded *adj.*	Zakhmī
Wise	Aqlmand	Wrap *v. tr.*	Lapētnā
Without	Kē baghair	Wrath	Ghussa *m.*
Witness	Gawāh *m.*	Wrist	Kalāī *f.*
Wolf	Bhēṛiā *m.*	Write	Likhnā
Wonder *v. tr.*	Ta'ajjub *k.*	Wrong *adj.*	Ghalat
Wonderful *adj.*	Ajib		
Wood	Lakrī *f.*		

Y

Yard	Gaz	Yet	Abhi tak;
Year	Saal		Phir bhī
Yearly *adv.*	Har sāl	Yoke	Jūā *m.*
Yellow *adj.*	Pīlā; zard	Yoke *v. tr.*	Jotnā
Yesterday	Kal	Young	Jawān
		Youth	Jawānī *f.*

Z

Zeal	Sargarmi *f.*	Zigzag	Pēchdār;
Zealous *adj.*	Sargarm		Mor tor ke
		Zinc	Jast *m.*